Taekwondo Poomsae: The Fighting Scrolls
Guiding Philosophy and Basic Applications

By Kingsley Umoh

Strategic Book Publishing and Rights Co.

Strategic Book Publishing and Rights Co.
12620 FM 1960, Suite A4-507
Houston, TX 77065
www.sbpra.com

ISBN: 978-1-61204-801-7

Book Design: Suzanne Kelly

Dedication

This book is dedicated to my parents, Akpan Johnny Umoh and Ekaette Akpan Umoh for their steadfast love and belief in me, to my wife Patricia and children Enobong and Sunil for being able to draw smiles from me even in my moments of frustration, and to the millions of others in the Taekwondo family who find the energy regularly to go through yet another day's hard physical training.

About the Author

Kingsley Ubong Umoh was only fourteen when he took his first step from being an ardent fan of the Hong Kong Kung Fu movies into the practical world of Taekwondo Jidokwan training in the early 1980s. As most inveterate martial artists would discover, the exciting world of flying kicks and somersaults was very different from the hardships of intense training so difficult that it would sometimes appear that the master was actively trying to discourage his students from continuing further classes.

Thus was taught the first lesson of perseverance and indomitable spirit. He counts himself fortunate to have trained variously with different instructors to achieve different perspectives which are important to round out one's knowledge of Taekwondo. To this day, it is his firm conviction that the serious student of the Korean martial arts must avail himself or herself the knowledge and wisdom of more than one teacher.

After graduating from high school, Umoh gained admission into the University of Ibadan in Nigeria to study medicine in 1984. He quickly located the university's Taekwondo club and restarted his training. To his surprise and chagrin, his yellow belt which had been achieved through a double promotion wasn't recognized in his new club and he had to join the ranks of the beginners. This was a blessing in disguise, as he was being taught important lessons in humility.

He continued to train regularly, always looking forward to the next class. During holidays while his peers were mostly engaged in other leisurely activities, he would continue his training at two separate clubs in Lagos, the old capital city. In no time, he developed more skills and became the senior student at his university club, even as others dropped out, ultimately achieving his first dan black belt in 1988.

Taekwondo was undergoing a revolution at this time with its inclusion into the Olympic Games, and like thousands of students he harbored dreams of competing at that elite level, but this was not to be his destiny. He soon graduated as a doctor in 1990.

His interest in literature was firmly established in childhood, as he was usually found devouring novels and encyclopedia. An example of his early interest in writing came when he created a manual of poomsae with the erstwhile aim of assisting his fellow university students which was never published. However, the germ of this idea remained buried within him until now.

As a junior medical doctor, the pressures of caring for the sick and raising a family deviated Umoh's attentions from a competition career in Taekwondo, aligning him on a different path. Rather than being a source of frustration, it opened new doors into his study of Taekwondo. He began to query his previous understanding of the martial arts, embarking on a road less travelled at that time.

This book is the product of research into the guiding philosophy and techniques of Taekwondo; an effort to broaden the scope of the serious student of the martial arts to achieve a fuller appreciation of training in all aspects of the Korean martial arts. It is a book he wishes he had written more than two decades ago.

Contents

Acknowledgement

The journey of a thousand miles begins with the first step. To the following people I express deep gratitude for their untiring effort and assistance extended to me during the course of my Taekwondo journey.

Master George Ashiru of the Nigerian Taekwondo Federation, thank you very much for showing me the first step and for remaining a bright star that cannot be dimmed. A special acknowledgement goes to Master Famous Dally for holding my hand all the way, ensuring I had a firm footing in this remarkable Korean art of self-defense. I shall never forget Grandmaster Emmanuel Ikpeme and Benson, who gave me several valuable lessons for free. I have tried to follow in your footsteps.

In the second half of this journey, highest regards go to Masters Conrad Jenkins, Christopher Chok, and Paul Lindo of the Jamaican Taekwondo Federation as well as Master Steve Graham from the Cayman Islands for rekindling the fire inside me when I reached that crossroad in life. This book has come as a direct result of my rebirth.

Even at this late stage, I remain indebted to Grandmaster Hock Lye Ooi from Canada for being forthright in his answers to some difficult questions and for improving my Taekwondo.

To my children, Enobong and Sunil, I owe a lot of my insight into the hieroglyphics of the martial arts. They have served as eager models at all hours of the day, even as I worked out the various holds and locks concealed within the different poomsae sequences.

Special thanks to Jason Carpenter, Rory Young, Rochelle Clarke, Shavanory Green, Lanique Smith, Lipton Lee and Swashnair Dixon for sacrificing your time to assist me in the long hours it took to photograph the different techniques. I commend you all for refusing to complain despite the harsh weather, hard blows, and heavy falls.

Final thanks to the members of the Korea Taekwondo Association Poomsae Committee, without whom it would have been impossible to undertake the task of this book. Every time I discover a new application to a technique, I am reminded how much more there is to know, and can better appreciate the hard work that went into composing the various patterns.

To all students and practitioners of Taekwondo, I wish you greater wisdom as you continue the development of our martial art.

Taekwondo Poomsae: The Fighting Scrolls

CHAPTER I

Yin and Yang

The year is 1965, the Chinese Year of the Snake, and inside a corner of Southeast Asia several battles rage simultaneously. To be more precise, South Vietnam is locked in a series of deadly battles against determined rebels supported by its North Vietnamese enemy. The south is amply supported by arms and men from the United States and its allies, like the South Korean government. And blood flows like red wine from an uncorked bottle.

Millions of people are born that year in other parts of the world. According to Chinese horology, they are considered Snake people—intuitive, introspective, exciting, refined, and dark at the same time. Such people are blessed with the ability to read complex situations quickly and act with speed and when faced with a dilemma. The ability to judge situations correctly and confidently often lead many to become thinkers and philosophers.

Hundreds of miles away in another corner of Northeast Asia, the sun pours down its heated rays on Seoul, the capital of the Republic of Korea, and its government, ruled by General Park Chung-hee, the erstwhile strongman and friend of the White House. It is summertime and peace reigns in this part of the Korean peninsula.

The martial arts leader glances down on the papers in front of him, then adjusts his sixties-style glasses with their broad rims, squinting through them. He is Grandmaster Lee, a ninth dan black belt born in the Year of the Snake and a senior member of one of the *kwans* or martial arts gyms. Around him are seated other senior martial arts leaders, members of the testing committee of the Korean Taekwondo Association, facing nervous-looking candidates for the various ranks of the black belt. At this point, Taekwondo is still fragmented into at least nine separate *kwans*. It will take another decade to finally merge theses competing styles into a uniquely Korean fighting style, and ultimately achieve success as the most popular martial art in the world.

Each candidate is expected to demonstrate two patterns appropriate for their intended rank to the committee. There are many styles of Taekwondo, most practicing different sets of *hyungs* or patterns, the majority of which originated from abroad in places like China and Japan. The list of patterns is long, made to accommodate and include the teachings of the nine *kwans*. The senior grandmaster looks down on his papers again.

Requirements for the first degree black belt:

Included in this list is General Choi, Hong Hi's *Hwarang Hyung*, celebrating the elite warriors of the ancient Silla kingdom of Korea, otherwise called the Hwarang. It is part of the twenty-four patterns or *tuls* created by one of the most important of modern Taekwondo's founders. The rest are of foreign origin.

The five Pyongan Hyungs or Pinan kata are: Chodan, Idan, Samdan, Sadan, and Odan. Pinan ("Peaceful Mind") is also known as Heians by the Shotokan in Japan but was developed from Channan, an old, forgotten Chinese form by the Anko Itosu, the great Okinawan Shorin-ryu master. These forms serve to gradually introduce more difficult techniques to the advancing student.

Naebojin Chodan Hyung is the first of the original three Okinawan Naihanchi kata series. Meaning "Iron Horse" or "Staying and Fighting," it stresses the development of fighting ki. It was popularized by another great Okinawan master, Choki Motubu, and its beginnings are buried in its Shaolin Kung Fu past.

Chul Ki Hyung Chodan is also known as Naihanchi kata or Tekki Sho, the later Shotokan version.

Ja Won Hyung or Jion, another Shorin-ryu kata, conceals a fierce fighting spirit within its smooth movements.

Requirements for the second degree black belt:

Naebojin Idan Hyung is the second in the Naihanchi or "Iron Horse" set of forms from the Shorin-ryu. Kima Idan Hyung and Shotokan's Tekki Nidan are close versions of this Naihanchi kata.

Chong Moo Hyung is a creation of Choi, Hong Hi, naming it after Admiral Sun Shin Yi, Korea's foremost naval tactician and one of the ancient world's greatest.

Requirements for the third degree black belt:

Ul- Ji and Ge- Baek Hyung are named after important generals in old Korean history as part of the twenty-four Chang Hon tuls of Choi, Hong Hi.

Pal Saek Hyung, otherwise called Bassai, is one of four forms devised by an early Okinawan master named Kosaku Matsumora. Its name can be interpreted to mean "to penetrate the fortress" and it teaches various escapes, blocks, and counters to surmount an adverse situation and wrest victory.

No Pae Hyung or Ro Hai ("Sign of the White Heron") is traced to Matsumora, who brought it from China. It featured a one-foot stance to symbolize a crane standing on a rock, and it includes sweeps and throwing techniques.

Another form on this list is Dan Kwon Hyung, with origins in Shaolin Kung Fu.

Yon Bi Hyung, otherwise called Wanshu in Okinawa, or Empi kata, Japan's version, emphasizes nimble body motions and swift reversal of body movements similar to the flight of a swallow.

Requirements for the fourth degree black belt:

Naebojin Samdan Hyung is the third of the Naihanchi or "Iron Horse" forms beloved by Choki Motubu, who believed that mastering it allowed the practitioner to develop and excel in the martial arts. Kima Samdan Hyung is a version of this third "Iron Horse" pattern.

Am Hak Hyung or Jindo Hyung or Chinto, meaning "Fighting Techniques from the East," is an advanced Shudokan karate kata of Shorin-ryu lineage, traced to Bushi Matsumura, the bodyguard to the Okinawan king, who in turn learned it from a Chinese seaman stranded on the shores of Okinawa. It makes extensive use of the one-legged stance of the crane and also teaches hand trapping and breaking.

Other patterns in the curriculum of the Shudokan founder Toyama Kanken are Ja Un Hyung, Jin Soo Hyung, and Chul Ki Samdan Hyung .

Sam Il Hyung is General Choi's creation, containing thirty-three movements to symbolize the thirty-three patriots who planned the independence movement to resist the Japanese Occupation forces in 1919.

So Rim Jang Kwon Hyung is a version of the Shaolin Long Fist form.

Requirements for the fifth degree black belt:

Kong Sang Kun Hyung or Kusanku includes elements of techniques taught to Tode Sakugawa by Kusanku, the Chinese official to the Royal Court of Okinawa. It includes many grappling methods.

Kwan Kong Hyung is another form that originated from Kusanku's teachings.

Ship Soo Hyung or Jitte in Japanese is a Shudokan kata meaning "Ten Hands" and it can also be performed with a weapon like the staff. It is said to allow one to perform the actions of ten men while facing attacks from multiple directions.

Oh Ship Sabo Hyung or Gojushiho ("Fifty-four Steps of the Black Tiger") is a form practiced by the Shudokan of Toyama Kanken and contains a lot of techniques from Chinese Kung Fu within its seventy-seven steps encompassing a range of circular theory techniques, and super-fast and slow attacks that utilize the neck movements of the crane and its beak.

Ban Wol Hyung is another form from the Shudokan's Shorin-ryu lineage.

The last one on the list is Pal Ki Kwon Hyung, also of Chinese origin.

He glances again at the nervous-looking candidates. This would be the last time any black belt candidate would be performing these patterns in front of him. They had been made obsolete almost overnight by the newer set of Hyung created by the Korean Taekwondo Association Poomsae Committee, and it was scheduled to be released in various training clinics the following year. These would subsequently be called Poomsae and would be based on the *palgwe* or eight kwae to reflect their Korean origin and pride.

Today in the group of senior leaders he has spotted only two or three of the masters tasked with the creation of these uniquely Korean forms. He knows each member well and his heart warms up at the thought of the coming changes that will rock the world of Taekwondo. At the moment the nine committee members are perhaps the most important men of Taekwondo. They are Hyun Jong Myun, the second headmaster of the Oh Do Kwan; Lee Kyo Yoon, the founder of the Han Moo Kwan; Kim Soon Bae, the third headmaster of the Chang Moo Kwan; Kwak Kun Sik, twelfth black belt graduate of the Chung Do Kwan; Park Hae Man, senior black belt student of Uhm Woon Kyu, headmaster of the Chung Do Kwan; Lee Yong Sup, the second headmaster of the Song Moo Kwan; Lee Chong Woo, the second headmaster of the Ji Do Kwan; Han Young Tae, senior black belt student of Hwang Kee, the founder of the Moo Duk Kwan; and Bae Young Ki, the third headmaster of the Ji Do Kwan.

Within his mind, he contemplates the finer points each candidate must demonstrate when performing each form; an expression of their understanding and ability to use the techniques as an effective training tool for fighting the external and internal battles.

The student must remain calm during the performance of the Hyung. He or she must begin and end each form on the same spot. He or she must execute each technique smoothly and completely before moving on to the next move. He or she must maintain the correct posture and balance when moving through the stances in each Hyung. The student must breathe deeply using the diaphragm, expanding the body by relaxing and uncoiling during inspiration. Then he or she must contract the body at the end of each technique during expiration, adding snap and explosiveness to forcefully release great energy in the execution of the technique. The student must use the correct speed and power according to the tempo of each form. He or she must maintain eye contact and concentration on an imaginary target. He or she must kihap vigorously to release the energy from the Danjun at the appropriate point in each Hyung. Finally, the student must know the meaning and philosophy underlying each Hyung.

Fast forward two decades, and the patterns are now fully Korean, are called poomsae, and start with the Taegeuk. They differ from the older Chinese and Okinawan forms chiefly in the mode of attacking the body's various vital points, relying heavily on the one strike-one kill philosophy of self-defense. *Taegeuk has no form, no beginning and no end...* declared the Samil Sinko, the Scripture of the Korean Race, the "Korean bible."

These words echo in his head, reverberating and releasing the distant faded memory of the old Buddhist monk who had taught him Kong Soo Do secretly in a monastery many years ago in what is present day North Korea. Then, it was still a single Korea under a brutal Japanese occupation. Even now, the monk's words are as crystal clear as when they were first uttered. "It is important to remember the philosophical trinity of the Taegeuk, Infinity, Um, and Yang."

Another set of nervous candidates await their turn to demonstrate their mastery of the new forms. Senior Grandmaster Park carefully studies the papers in his hands. He is a protégé of Grandmaster Lee, who passed away the previous year in his early seventies. He is also the head of four Taekwondo gyms in the downtown Chicago area which he started after emigrating to the U.S. in 1975.

Requirements for the First Dan Black Belt:

Palgwe Il Jang & Taegeuk Il Jang
Palgwe Ee Jang & Taegeuk Ee Jang
Palgwe Sam Jang & Taegeuk Sam Jang
Palgwe Sah Jang & Taegeuk Sah Jang
Palgwe Oh Jang & Taegeuk Oh Jang
Palgwe Yuk Jang & Taegeuk Yuk Jang
Palgwe Chil Jang & Taegeuk Chil Jang
Palgwe Pal Jang & Taegeuk Pal Jang

Grandmaster Park is the most senior of the examiners and has been accorded the privilege of heading the table. He looks up from his papers directly into the bright eyes of the teenage female second generation Korean-American aspirant for the third degree poom black belt who stands respectfully at attention only a few feet away. Faint beads of perspiration evaporate off her young face.

"What is the meaning of the Taegeuk?"

The answer pours out immediately. She is young and bright.

"The Taegeuk is the symbol of the universe or cosmos. It is a compound word used to represent the supreme ultimate, with Tae meaning 'bigness' while Geuk means 'eternity.' This is the supreme law that governs all the forces in our universe, including Taekwondo. In Taekwondo Poomsae, the Taegeuk is comprised of a female half, of forces of negative energy commonly called the Yin or Um in Korea, which represent passive, contracting, soft, yielding qualities. These are held in balance by the Yang or male half, of positive attributes such as active, expanding, hard, aggressive energy. These opposing yet complementary Yin and Yang forces are enclosed within one bubble or sphere as represented by the circle of the Taegeuk. The central sine-wave line that divides this circle creates a top half representing Yang, conventionally depicted in red color, and a bottom half of Yin in blue color. It shows the relationship between the opposing forces which are interdependent on each other, meaning that when Yin becomes dominant it will ultimately transform into Yang, and the opposite is true for Yang when it becomes Yin."

The senior grandmaster's eyes brighten as he listens.

"This sine wave line also represents the ki force or universal energy as a constant and shows how it circulates within every living being or inanimate object, transforming from positive Yang force to negative Yin force. Surrounding the circle are eight trigrams or Palgwe with opposing pairs directly across each other. These are composed of combinations of either straight bars representing Yang or divided bars representing Yin. The Palgwe represent the 'Law or Command' of the Taegeuk and are specifically placed opposite each other to indicate the different possibilities the Taekwondo student may face at each point in time."

She is confident in her knowledge.

"The arrangement of the Taegeuk was set out by the great Korean philosopher Sinsi Bonki, a son of the fifth emperor of the Hwan-ung Dynasty around 35 B.C., who claimed to have glimpsed the rituals of Heaven, receiving afterward the eight kwae. Deeper meaning of the relationship between the Yang and Yin forces and the trigrams are taken from an equally ancient text known as the Book of Changes called the Joo-Yeok in Korea or the I'Ching by the Chinese."

The senior grandmaster presses her further.

"What do you know of the Book of Changes?"

"This was compiled 5,000 years ago in China by the Zhou people. It was written during the Shang Dynasty at a time of great upheaval. The ruling family had forfeited Heaven's Mandate to rule on account of their great corruption. King Wen of the Zhou was seen fit to receive the mandate and he led an army with his son Wu the Martial to overthrow the Shang Dynasty and install a new dynasty lasting 800 years.

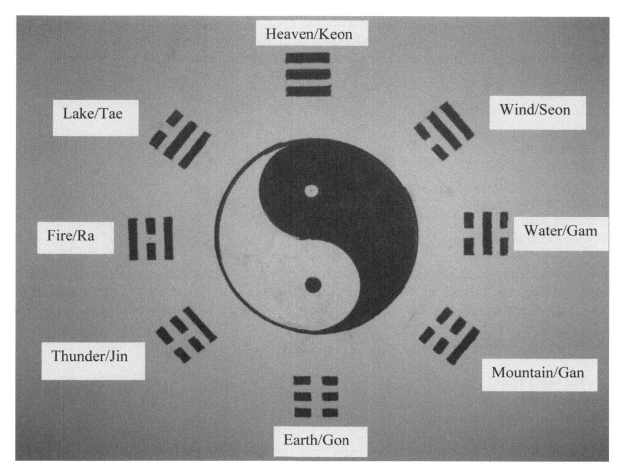

PICTURE 1
Palgwe Trigrams of the Taegeuk

The Joo-Yeok is useful as an oracle to divine answers to various problems. It is all encompassing and consists of sixty-four hexagrams which are created by a doubling of the trigrams in varying combinations."

A faint smile appeared on his lip. Many years ago he had also studied the texts. It was compulsory reading in his family and its words were vague and opaque then and made for difficult reading. Now there was greater clarity and wisdom with his old age.

I'CHING OR JOO-YEOK (BOOK OF CHANGES)

HEXAGRAM 1—Creative Force (Il Jang)

"Creative Force.
From the source, creating success.
Constancy bears fruit."
The movement of heaven
Is full of grand power.
Thus the superior man
Makes himself strong and tireless.

Il Jang as the first Taegeuk pattern represents the symbol of Keon, meaning the Heaven and Yang. Heaven is the father, found in the south, and symbolizes the beginning of the creation of all things in the universe. It is the realm between autumn and winter when the buds set and the seeds fall to the fertile soil.

HEXAGRAM 58—Opening (Ee Jang)
"Opening.
Creating success.
Constancy bears fruit."
Lakes resting on each other.
The image of the Joyous.
The superior man joins with his friends
For discussion and practice.

Ee Jang as the second Taegeuk pattern symbolizes the Tae or lake with its inner firmness and outer softness. It is also the youngest daughter, the joyful spirit of the fertile south east and of the autumn. Tae can be both soft or deceptively calming on the surface and hard with strong undercurrents below.

HEXAGRAM 30—Clarity (Sam Jang)
"Clarity.
Constancy bears fruit.
Creating success.
Raising female cattle is good fortune."

Sam Jang as the third Taegeuk pattern symbolizes the Ra, meaning hot and bright, the spirit of hot enthusiasm. It is the middle daughter living in the east. This is the region of the midsummer. It encourages the trainee to harbor a sense of justice and ardor for training. Ra is represented by fire, which can burn both slow and controlled or fast and uncontrollable.

HEXAGRAM 51—Shock (Sah Jang)
"Shock, creating success.
Shock comes, fear and terror.
Laughing words, shrieking and yelling.
Shock spreads fear for a hundred miles.
Someone does not lose the sacred ladle and libation."

Sah Jang as the fourth Taegeuk pattern symbolizes the Jin which represents the great power and dignity of thunder. It is also the eldest son, emerging into the field and starting to grow. Thunder is in the northeast and represents the spring. Thunder as the symbol of the fourth pattern is well known to exist in two forms: the initial one being the phase of gathering energy, followed by the second phase where the mighty energy is released.

HEXAGRAM 57—Subtly Penetrating (Oh Jang)
"Subtly penetrating, creating small success.
Fruitful to have a direction to go,
Fruitful to see the great person."

Oh Jang as the fifth Taegeuk pattern represents the Son, meaning the wind. This has mighty force and calmness according to its strength and weakness. The wind is the eldest daughter, gentle and submissive, belonging in the southwest, in the late spring and early summer. The phenomenon of the wind is also universally recognizable in two forms, existing as a gentle force or exhibiting great devastation as a hurricane. This duality is retained in the fifth poomsae.

HEXAGRAM 29—*Repeating Chasms (Yuk Jang)*

"Repeating chasms.
There is truth and confidence.
Holding your heart fast creates success.
Movement brings honour."

Yuk Jang as the sixth Taegeuk pattern represents the kam or water, meaning incessant flow and softness. It is the middle son found in the west. It is also symbolic of midwinter. The sixth pattern is represented by the water symbol which is present in lakes, streams, rivers, and seas. Water once it starts moving flows in two directions, forward and backward or retreating, to and fro, to make wave action.

HEXAGRAM 52—*Stilling (Chil Jang)*

"Stilling your back,
Not grasping yourself.
Moving in your rooms,
Not seeing your people.
Not a mistake.
Mountains standing close together.
The image of keeping still.
The superior man does not permit his thought
To go beyond his situation."

Chil Jang as the seventh Taegeuk pattern represents the kan or mountain. This means ponder and firmness. It is the youngest son, confident and of independent spirit, belonging in the northwest and late winter approaching spring. The seventh pattern is represented by the mighty mountain which is majestic in its solidity or unyielding nature, yet may be become yielding when it is split by a volcanic eruption.

HEXAGRAM 2—*Earth (Pal Jang)*

"Earth.
From the source, creating success.
The constancy of a mare bears fruit.
A noble one has a direction to go.
At first, confusion.
Later, gains a master.
Fruitful in the southwest, gaining partners.
In the northeast, losing partners.
Peaceful constancy brings good fortune.
The earth possesses receptive devotion.
The superior man carries the world
With his strength of character."

Pal Jang is the last Taegeuk pattern before the black belt, and represents Kon, which symbolizes earth and Yin. This is the mother and is found in the north .It stands for the root and settlement, the beginning and the end, the harvest time of late summer and early autumn.

The qualities of Yin and Yang are abundantly exemplified throughout the different Taegeuk and Palgwe patterns. The first poomsae is represented by "Heaven," implying only Yang qualities (offense, fast, powerful, hard, attacking, challenge, direct, strike, releasing energy, unyielding, linear, to separate, advancing, originating in the pores of the skin) or forces represented in the four extremities.

The eighth poomsae manifesting as "Earth" embraces the opposite and complimentary values of defensive, slowness, speed, softness, retreating, response, evade, grapple, gathering energy, yielding, circular, unite, and withdrawal. It is manifested in the lower orifices, or forces moving within the five solid organs of the heart, the lungs, the liver, the spleen, and the kidneys.

According to the Book of Changes, the creators of the Kwae are the two main forces, the Creative or Father and the Receptive or Mother. Father is "Keon" and "Heaven," while Mother is "Kon" and "Earth." A deeper examination of the Palgwe explain the creative roles of Keon as the Father and Heaven , and Kon as the Mother or Earth .

All three sons including the Thunder, Water, and Mountain are created from the Mother.

Mother seeks for the first time the power of the male in the trigram of "The Arousing" and receives the Eldest Son "Thunder." The change from Yin to Yang occurs at the lowest bar. Next the Middle Son "Water" is created in the trigram of "The Abysmal," when Yin changes to Yang in the middle bar. Keon passes on the linear attack trait to its offspring Water trigram in Taegeuk Yuk Jang. Similarly, this is not a strong Yang trait and the poomsae remains unchanged with Yin energy.

Then follows the Youngest Son "Mountain," in the trigram of "Keeping Still," where Yin changes to Yang in the upper bar. Keon imparts the hard unyielding principle to its offspring Mountain trigram in Taegeuk Chil Jang. Since this is not its most important element, Kan energy remains Yin in this poomsae.

It is the grappling quality or Hap, where one adheres to the opponent, that is the most important trait from Kon the Mother or Earth trigram. This is found in the first four steps of Taegeuk Chil Jang, Yuk Jang, and Oh Jang.

The most important trait from Keon is techniques that force away the opponent contained within the first four steps of Taegeuk Ee Jang, Sam Jang, and Sah Jang respectively, which are enough to emphasize their Yang nature.

The Father is the origin of the remaining three trigrams of the Palgwe. The male seeking for the first time the power of the female receives the Eldest Daughter, "The Wind," in the trigram of "The Gentle" when the upper bar changes from Yang to Yin.

In the trigram "The Clinging," the Middle Daughter (Fire) is created when the middle bar changes to Yin. Kon again imparts the circular flowing trait to the Fire trigram of Taegeuk Sam Jang, which is still insufficient to change its energy to Yin.

The Youngest Daughter ("Lake") is created in the trigram of "The Joyous" when the lowest bar changes to um. The Yu or soft yielding trait in the Lake trigram of Taegeuk Ee Jang doesn't change it from Yang, as this isn't the most important Yin characteristic.

The techniques of Taegeuk and Palgwe Il Jang are easily suited to a person with a large and powerful frame who disposes his or her opponent easily with overwhelming force. On the other hand, a smaller or weaker person will find the soft, yielding techniques of Taegeuk and Palgwe Pal Jang very useful to deflect attacks from a more powerful opponent adapting and using his or her strength to defeat him.

In any fight, there is no guarantee that one will always be the bigger, stronger fighter. Thus the practitioner should be adaptable, using tactics that exploit the opponent's perceived weakness. Victory will usually belong to the more skilled fighter.

CHAPTER 2

Yin and Yang

The year is 2003 and the female black belt is a seventh dan black belt, a mother of four and nearly twenty years older. She runs her own gym in Boston, Massachusetts. In her study of the Book of Changes, these words were all riddles and sounded enigmatic initially, the female master remembers. The thorough understanding of their meanings came much later. It is now her turn to question aspiring black belt candidates.

The male black belt student bows before her in deference, a young American college student in his early twenties. He sounds just as confident and well-informed as she had been. He attempts to explain the eight kwae of the Taegeuk in detail.

The Joo-Yeok or Book of Changes plays a very central role in the understanding of the Palgwe and Taegeuk poomsae. This is hinged on its primary role as an important divination tool for millions of Asians who have studied its set of six lines or hexagrams, providing accurate answers to questions posed by the suppliant individual. These responses are found within any of its sixty-four hexagrams, which may sometimes appear opaque and require careful reading to reveal their recommendations.

It is important that the chosen question be clear in the communication with the Joo-Yeok. A vaguely worded question is unlikely to elicit a clear answer which is easy to understand, particularly the questions that demand a "yes" or "no" response. Likewise, inquiring about two alternatives in the communication may make the answer impossible to understand.

In utilizing the Book of Changes to understand the philosophy of the Taegeuk or Palgwe poomsae, it is important that the correct question be posed. In Taekwondo practice, these inquiries concern tactics and strategies of fighting, and on a deeper level the spiritual connection to the cosmic energy of the universe.

Just like the senior grandmaster who had examined her two decades earlier, she is impressed at his understanding of this important piece of Asian culture.

There are three principles of Sam Jae, or the three elements forming the different levels of the trigrams. The first bar (which is really the lowest bar as you look from the periphery toward the center of the circle) represents Cheon or Heaven, the middle bar is In or Humanity, and the bottom bar, which is closest to the circle, is Ji or Earth.

Classical Taoist theory explains that the three levels are made up of the Heavens above and the Earth below, with Man in the middle as the conductor of life energy between both levels. It further describes the three treasures of the universe as Heaven, which is composed of its three treasures of the sun, the moon, and the stars; the Earth and its three treasures of air, fire, and water; and Mankind, with its three treasures of ki or life force energy, sexual energy, and the soul.

The Taegeuk is the manifestation of the principles of the cosmic creation and everything concerning human existence. Infinity is the unending nature of the Taegeuk contained within the circle, and Yin and Yang as negative and positive are separated from each other by the wave-like line of ki flow. These opposite but complementary poles symbolize the two forms of energy within the universe and are the embodiment of the inherent duality of human life.

"This line of ki is likened to the light rays which as white light pass through a prism or are refracted from the clouds on a rainy day and can separate into a rainbow of the primary colors. These include violet, indigo, blue, green, yellow, orange, and red. Just like the rainbow, these components of the ki energy can be described as starting from heavenly energy, before separating into the lake, fire, thunder, wind, water, and mountain energies, finally regrouping as earth energy. These phenomena are arranged as the eight sets of bars or Palgwe and represent vital elements in our world," he continues. "Just as in the Taegeuk, the Lake and the Mountain are part of the landscape, often existing together, and are both admired for their beauty and majesty. Their sum in the poomsae order (two plus seven) makes nine.

"Fire and Water are essential elements for survival and renewal of all living things, and their useful properties have been harnessed by mankind for ages in cooking meals. Their pairing as opposites in the Taegeuk is an acknowledgement of their intertwined roles in our lives. Their sum (three plus six) equals nine.

"The next complementary pair of Thunder and Wind acknowledge the vital forces of nature which shape the landscape and water, the great fertile plains. In fact, we would not be able to breathe oxygen-rich air if the wind was not present to replenish the vital air around us. Just as well, the thunder, though terrifying in its loudness, is welcomed by the agricultural fields as it brings needed rain. Their sum (four plus five) gives nine.

"Finally, Heaven and Earth cannot exist one without the other. They are both the greatest gifts of the creation from which all that exist in nature spring from. Their sum in the poomsae order (one plus eight) also equals nine.

"Thus at any point of the circle of the Taegeuk, irrespective of which way it is turned, the opposing pair of forces add up to nine. Therefore, the different Taegeuk and Palgwe poomsae may be regarded as separate chapters of a single long poomsae. The philosophy of the Taegeuk is the highest manifestation of training in Taekwondo and is derived from the influences of Daoism and Buddhist thought. The number nine is considered to be a celestial number and the supreme spiritual power. It can be broken down into a component set of three as the basic unit, and the triple levels of the Palgwe trigrams have been derived from this.

"Accordingly, Humanity is the conductor of life force between Heaven above and Earth below. Similarly, there are three energy centers or minds in the body, and these correspond to the different bars of the trigram. These are the Upper Danjun within the brain where the mind and spirit reside, the Middle Danjun where the emotional brain and soul reside within the heart, and the Lower Danjun located in the lower abdomen. These life-energy centers can store, transform, and channel vital energy to each other and other major organs including the spinal cord and the sexual organs."

"What about the five element theory?" she presses the young man.

"This is the theory of energy creation and nourishment. The universe is composed of the five essential elements of metal, water, wood, fire, and earth. The cycle of creation begins with metal giving birth to water, water creating wood, wood creating fire, fire creating earth, and earth creating metal. Likewise, there is the equally important cycle of destruction or energy regulation where metal destroys wood, wood destroys earth, earth destroys water, water destroys fire, and fire destroys metal.

"Il Jang and Ee Jang are patterns with manifestations of metal energy through the use of low narrow stances which are adaptable and efficient in grappling. The metal element represents the lungs and the large intestine and the practice of these patterns promotes the movement of the ki energy through the body by improving the functions of these organs. Yuk Jang reflects water energy which is feminine and yielding, including techniques which are both encircling and deceptively powerful. The water element is related to the function of the kidneys in eliminating the waste fluids. This pattern enhances the water metabolism through movements that create torsion of the body and massage the kidneys. Sah Jang and Oh Jang are full of wood energy and represent movement with footwork and techniques that incorporate the movement of a gentle breeze or gale wind. Wood energy is related to the liver and gall bladder and regulate the storage of blood and flow of ki.

"Sam Jang manifests radiating fire or masculine energy with forceful techniques that are penetrating and explosive. The heart and the small intestine are regulated by fire energy to improve the overall circulation and digestion of food. Chil Jang and Pal Jang both consist of earth energy and stable, low wide stances

PICTURE 2
Yin or Um Trigram

suitable for grappling and ground-fighting. Earth energy is related to the spleen and stomach which are responsible for clear thinking and digestion."

"What kinds of poomsae techniques do you know?" she queries him.

The Taegeuk and Palgwe poomsae can be interpreted based on three useful criteria applied to the bars of each trigram. For the patterns manifesting Yin energy, these attributes are listed below:

The Yu element in the outer bar are soft and yielding techniques.

The Won element in the middle bar are flowing circular techniques.

The Hap element in the inner bar are movements that close the space between both opponents such as grappling and clinching techniques. This last level is the most important characteristic of the poomsae determining its Yin character.

The character of the yang energy patterns are also described in like manner with three other principles, starting from the upper bar to the lowest bar as following:

The Kang element in the outer bar represents hard and unyielding techniques.

The Kok element in the middle bar represents linear or angular techniques.

The Kan element in the inner bar represents striking techniques that force the distance between both fighters by knocking the opponent away. This feature is the most important characteristic that infuses the pattern with Yang energy.

PICTURE 3
Yang Trigram

It is important to recognize the underlying differences between the Taegeuk and Palgwe poomsae. There is a common misconception that the Palgwe poomsae were derived solely from Japanese or Okinawan karate as opposed to the Korean origins of the Taegeuk poomsae, that the Palgwe forms were discontinued to allow for the nationalist Korean character to be manifest in the subsequent Taegeuk series. If that reasoning was correct, then the black belt set of poomsae which tend to have a closer family resemblance to the Palgwe should have been replaced wholesale.

The Taegeuk forms focus the student's attention on the important role stances play in the successful execution of techniques. There is a differentiation between the stances and transitional body positions that represent forward motion, retreat, or static position. In turn, the shifting center of gravity and balance of the student allows for full control and domination of the opponent.

The more advanced Taegeuk poomsae include sequences in which the student is introduced early to the concept of dynamic tension and chi energy concentration and movement. This training theory is also utilized in the black belt poomsae but absent in the Palgwe set.

In addition, the Taegeuk forms focus on economy of movement where the opponent is controlled using a minimum of steps or forward movement. These tactics would be important in fights involving confined spaces and surroundings filled with different obstacles.

Finally, the common use of the upright fighting stance of the Taegeuk patterns is reflective of the common self-defense scenario on the streets. The fight usually comes with the martial artist standing upright on both feet and unprepared to drop into a deeper defensive stance. Here the benefits from mobility and swift evasion are often prized higher than lower stable stances. This is an overturning of the usual triumph of form over function.

In spite of the above differences between the two sets of pre-black belt poomsae, the Book of Changes in its responses has influenced the fighting tactics found within their sequences. The principles behind the answers from the Joo-Yeok have common application to the Palgwe and Taegeuk forms.

CHAPTER 3

Poomsae Taegeuk and Palgwe

SELF-DEFENSE QUESTION 1: Response to an attack from the front.

TAEGEUK IL JANG vs. TAEGEUK PAL JANG
POOM EXERCISE NO. 1 (YANG)
Taegeuk Il Jang—Steps 13 & 14: Offensive techniques that knock the opponent aside (Heaven)

Turn left and thrust your left forearm upward from below to break his grip. Knock him backward with a strong kick. Finish him with a devastating fist strike.

POOM EXERCISE NO. 2 (UM/YIN)
Taegeuk Pal Jang—Steps 20–23: Use opponent's power against him (Earth)

Turn left and break his hold with your sweeping left palm trapping his left wrist in turn. Then twist his left arm counterclockwise and push your right elbow against the back of his arm. Apply an elbow lock by cranking his arm clockwise behind him. Push his elbow forward with your left hand sending him tumbling to the ground.

PALGWE IL JANG vs. PALGWE PAL JANG

POOM EXERCISE NO. 3 (YANG)

Palgwe Il Jang—Steps 5–8: Incessant offense to drive opponent back (Heaven)

Turn left and break his hold with your left hand. Smash your right hammer-fist into his left side. Then strike his spine with your left elbow. Knock him out with a powerful punch to the head.

POOM EXERCISE NO. 4 (UM/YIN)
Palgwe Pal Jang—Steps 7–10: Upset opponent's balance and draw him into your strike (Earth)

Turn left and break his hold by swinging both hands to your right to clear his left arm. Trap his left forearm and strike his neck with your left knife-hand. Use both hands to force his left arm behind his back in a chicken wing shoulder lock.

A second opponent seizes and pulls your outstretched right hand to free his friend. Twist your right arm behind your back and spin around, whipping your left back fist into his face. Finish him off with a powerful punch to the body.

NOTES

_____

_____

_____

_____

_____

_____

_____

_____

_____

_____

_____

_____

TAEGEUK EE JANG vs. TAEGEUK CHIL JANG

POOM EXERCISE NO. 5 (YANG)

Taegeuk Chil Jang—Steps 14–16: Clinch with and knock down the opponent (Mountain)

Break his double grip with both hands and step inside to penetrate his defenses. Grab his shoulders and pull his head down into your knee strike . Cross both hands behind his head and step backward, smashing his face down on your knee.

POOM EXERCISE NO. 6 (UM/YIN)

Taegeuk Ee Jang—Step 13: Drop your weight to break opponent's grip (Lake)

Turn left and swing your right forearm over his hands. Push downward to break his hold.

NOTES

_____

_____

_____

_____

_____

_____

_____

_____

_____

PALGWE EE JANG vs. PALGWE CHIL JANG

POOM EXERCISE NO. 7 (YANG)

Palgwe Chil Jang—Steps 1–4: Defensive joint locks and aggressive strikes (Mountain)

Bring both arms to the center and force your elbows down on his arms to break his hold. Seize his hands, pulling them apart to either side. Strike his groin with your front kick and crank his wrists to apply elbow locks. Smash your left front kick into his lower belly and cross your hands above to crank his wrists further. Knock him down by thrusting your side-kick to crush his knees. Jerk his right arm forward and strike his neck with your right knife-hand to knock him out.

NOTES

POOM EXERCISE NO. 8 (UM/YIN)
Palgwe Ee Jang—Steps 5–8: Immobilize opponent followed by forward takedown (Lake)

Break his hold and turn left, trapping his left arm against your body with your right hand. Force him down by pushing your left knife-hand down against the back of his arm. Step in gripping his left elbow and force his hand up his back. Push his left elbow upward, making his head and shoulder drop below your waist. Step forward and knock him down with a push from behind.

TAEGEUK SAM JANG vs. TAEGEUK YUK JANG

POOM EXERCISE NO. 9 (YANG)

Taegeuk Sam Jang—Steps 13 & 14: Enter opponent's cave and break his defenses (Fire)

Turn left and force his hand down by twisting his wrist to break his hold. Finish him off with a kick and double fist strikes.

POOM EXERCISE NO. 10 (UM/YIN)
Taegeuk Yuk Jang—Steps 14 & 15: Use defensive techniques to stick to opponent (Water)

Turn left and grab his left hand pulling it down to break his hold. Then force his hand to bend, twisting it clockwise to apply a wrist lock and kick his mid-section. Grip his left shoulder with your left hand with your forearm as a fulcrum under his left arm. Drop your weight backward to apply an arm bar.

PALGWE SAM JANG vs. PALGWE YUK JANG

POOM EXERCISE NO. 11 (YANG)

Palgwe Sam Jang—Steps 5–8: Focus your strikes at opponent's head to destabilize him (Fire)

Turn left and break his hold by pulling his left hand down and applying a wrist lock. Step forward again, thrusting your right elbow up into the side of his head. With a third forward step smash your left forearm into his jaw. Finish him off with a piercing solar plexus strike.

POOM EXERCISE NO. 12 (UM/YIN)
Palgwe Yuk Jang—Steps 5–7: Flow with opponent and overcome him on the ground (Water)

Turn left and break his hold by pulling his left hand down and applying a wrist lock. Block his right hand swing with your left palm-edge and strike his neck with your right knife-hand. Smash your right front kick into his groin, dropping him on his back. Pin him down with your right knee pushing into his side and apply both a wrist lock and armbar to his right arm. Drop your weight and wrench his arm clockwise with both hands to break his elbow.

TAEGEUK SAH JANG vs. TAEGEUK OH JANG

POOM EXERCISE NO. 13 (YANG)

Taegeuk Oh Jang—Steps 13–16: Apply forceful techniques to penetrate opponent's core (Wind)

Turn left and apply a wrist lock to his left hand to break his grip. Smash your right hammer-fist down into the back of his arm. Kick his groin and force him down with your right arm against his back, then smash your elbow into his spine. Turn left and push your left forearm under his left elbow to apply an arm bar. Then strike his head and attack his leg with your kick dropping him on his knees. Grab his head and swing your elbow into his face.

POOM EXERCISE NO. 14 (UM/YIN)

Taegeuk Sah Jang—Steps 13–16: Adhere to opponent and shock him with powerful strikes (Thunder)

Step forwards blocking his right hand at the wrist with an upward sweep of your left palm. Then strike his neck with your knife-hand. Kick his groin and smash your right elbow into his back. Twist his left arm anticlockwise and apply an arm bar with your right fore-arm. Crank his arm behind his back with your right hand, forcing him to bend down. Shift behind him and immobilize him by pushing his wrist up his back in a chicken wing shoulder lock.

NOTES

_____

_____

_____

_____

_____

_____

_____

_____

_____

_____

_____

PALGWE SAH JANG vs. PALGWE OH JANG

Poom Exercise No. 15 (YANG)
Palgwe Oh Jang—Steps 10–13: Apply gale-like force and push opponent back (Wind)

Turn left dropping your left fore-arm down on his right hand and push your right fore-arm upwards against his left hand before cranking both hands in opposite directions to break his double grip. Step forward again, twisting his right arm in both hands behind his back to damage his elbow. Step behind him and crank his right hand up to the back of his left shoulder. Damage his right shoulder by pushing his elbow forwards in the "V" of your right spear-hand.

POOM EXERCISE NO. 16 (UM/YIN)

Palgwe Sah Jang—Steps 7–10: Use abrupt changes in direction to shock and overcome the opponent (Thunder)

Break his hold and turn left, trapping his left arm with your right palm against your body. Strike his neck with your left knife-hand. Kick him in the chest and use both hands to force his left arm behind his back. Subdue him with a chicken wing shoulder lock.

A second opponent seizes your outstretched hand, pulling you forward. Twist your right arm behind your back to break free. Spin around and swing your left hammer-fist at his head. Finish him with a powerful strike to the body.

NOTES

_____

_____

_____

_____

_____

_____

_____

_____

_____

_____

_____

_____

CHAPTER 4

Poomsae Taegeuk and Palgwe

SELF-DEFENSE QUESTION 2: Response against an attack from the side.

TAEGEUK IL JANG vs. TAEGEUK PAL JANG

Poom Exercise No. 17 (YANG)
Taegeuk Il Jang—Steps 1 & 2: Knock opponent back with hard strikes (Heaven)

Break his grip by smashing your left hammer-fist into his groin. Then turn left to step behind him and shock him with a powerful strike to his kidneys.

POOM EXERCISE NO. 18 (UM/YIN)
Taegeuk Pal Jang—Steps 5 & 6: Adhere to opponent and apply defensive joint locks (Earth)

Force his hands apart to break his hold. Then step behind him and twist his right arm behind his back. Restrain him by wrapping your left forearm around his throat and push his hand up his shoulder.

PALGWE IL JANG vs. PALGWE PAL JANG

Poom Exercise No. 19 (YANG)

Palgwe Il Jang—Steps 9 & 10: Seize opponent and attack with great force (Heaven)

Slip your left leg around him and twist his right arm behind his back. Step forward, forcing him down and smash your right elbow downward into his spine.

POOM EXERCISE NO. 20 (UM/YIN)
Palgwe Pal Jang—Steps 11-15: Adhere to opponent and apply defensive joint locks (Earth)

Slip your left leg behind to obstruct his legs and strike his neck with your left knife-hand. Then swing your left fore-arm over his shoulder in a downward arc folding your elbow to press his right arm forwards and unbalance him before pulling back with your elbow strike to his ribs. Crank his right arm anti-clockwise behind his back and push his shoulder with your right hand, knocking him to the ground.

NOTES

_____

_____

_____

_____

_____

_____

_____

_____

_____

_____

_____

_____

_____

TAEGEUK EE JANG vs. TAEGEUK CHIL JANG

Poom Exercise No. 21 (YANG)

Taegeuk Ee Jang—Steps 1 & 2: Use forward momentum to defeat the opponent (Lake)

Break his grip by smashing your left hammer-fist into his groin. Then turn behind him and obstruct his left foot with your right leg . Push with your right hand using your momentum to knock him down in a forwards takedown.

POOM EXERCISE NO. 22 (UM/YIN)

Taegeuk Chil Jang—Steps 1 & 2: Control the opponent on the spot (Mountain)

Turn left to and slap his groin with your right hand to break his grip. Strike his chest with your right knee and smash your left elbow down on his spine.

PALGWE EE JANG vs. PALGWE CHIL JANG

Poom Exercise No. 23 (YANG)

Palgwe Ee Jang—Steps 9 &10: Use aggressive forward momentum to overcome the opponent (Lake)

Slip your leg behind him, smash your left fist into his groin to break his hold. Thrust your left fore-arm into his chest knocking him backwards. Then end the fight with a powerful kick and punch.

POOM EXERCISE NO. 24 (UM/YIN)

Palgwe Chil Jang—Steps 5–9: Use stable stances to adhere to and force opponent to the ground (Mountain)

Step behind him, scooping his right leg up in your left arm. Push his upper body backward with your right hand to unbalance him. Lift his right leg higher and kick his knee. Then apply an arm-bar with your right palm forcing him down. Finish the fight with a left hand punch to his head.

NOTES

_____

_____

_____

_____

_____

_____

_____

_____

_____

_____

_____

_____

_____

_____

_____

TAEGEUK SAM JANG vs. TAEGEUK YUK JANG

Poom Exercise No. 25 (YANG)

Taegeuk Sam Jang—Steps 1 & 2: Apply hard unyielding counter-attack (Fire)

Break his grip by smashing your left hammer-fist into his groin. Then strike his jaw with your right front kick. Finish him off with two punches to the ribs.

POOM EXERCISE NO. 26 (UM/YIN)
Taegeuk Yuk Jang—Steps 1 & 2: Overwhelm opponent's resistance before applying joint locks (Water)

Turn left to face him and break his grip by smashing your left hammer-fist into his groin. Strike his jaw with your right front kick to drop him on one knee. Push your left hand under his right arm to grab the front of his shirt. Twist his right arm anti-clockwise and lean back on it to apply an arm bar.

PALGWE SAM JANG vs. PALGWE YUK JANG

Poom Exercise No. 27 (YANG)

Palgwe Sam Jang—Steps 9 & 10: Seize the opponent and counter-attack with chops (Fire)

Slip around him and twist his right arm behind his back. Force him forward and strike the back of his head with your right knife-hand.

POOM EXERCISE NO. 28 (UM/YIN)

Palgwe Yuk Jang—Steps 8–10: Overwhelm opponent's resistance before applying joint locks (Water)

Slip behind him and strike his groin with your left hand and scoop his right leg up pushing his hip down to unbalance him. Thrust your hands between his arms and force them apart to break his hold and kick his groin. Push his left hand upward and backward over his left shoulder with your right hand. Crank his elbow upward with your left hand, pulling his wrist down in a rear takedown to the ground.

NOTES

_____

_____

_____

_____

_____

_____

_____

_____

_____

_____

_____

_____

_____

_____

TAEGEUK SAH JANG vs. TAEGEUK OH JANG

Poom Exercise No. 29 (YANG)

Taegeuk Sah Jang—Steps 1 & 2: Push forcefully through the opponent's defenses (Thunder)

Smash your left hand into his groin to break his grip. Seize his right arm, twisting it behind his back. With your left palm, pin his right hand into his back and force him on his knees. Step forward, pushing his elbow in the "V" of your right spear-hand to damage his shoulder and force him to the ground.

POOM EXERCISE NO. 30 (UM/YIN)
Taegeuk Oh Jang—Steps 1 & 2: Sweep the opponent off his feet like a whirlwind (Wind)

Step behind with your left foot outside his left foot and smash your left fist into his groin. Then under-hook the crook of your left elbow behind his right knee. Knock him down by scooping his right leg upward. Swing your left fist down on his falling body like the slicing blade of a windmill.

PALGWE SAH JANG vs. PALGWE OH JANG

Poom Exercise No. 31 (YANG)

Palgwe Sah Jang—Steps 11–13: Maintain offensive while withdrawing with the opponent (Thunder)

Smash your left hand into his groin to weaken his hold and step behind him .Break his grip by pushing both arms upward between his. Then pull his head down into your right uppercut punch to his jaw. Strike his face with your left knife-hand and sweep his leg, knocking him to the ground.

POOM EXERCISE NO. 32 (UM/YIN)

Palgwe Oh Jang—Steps 14–18: Suck the opponent up like a tornado and knock him to the ground (Wind)

Step behind him and break his hold by cranking his right arm anti-clockwise. Twist his right arm behind him in a shoulder lock by pushing his elbow with your right hand. Punch his kidneys with both fists and kick the back of his knee, dropping him on his knees. As he drops, smash the back of his head with your left hammer-fist and your right elbow. Mount his back and pull his collar backward tightly against his neck using your left hand. Reinforce the choke by pushing his head forward with your right palm.

NOTES

_____

_____

_____

_____

_____

_____

_____

_____

CHAPTER 5

Poomsae Taegeuk and Palgwe

SELF-DEFENSE QUESTION 3: Response against an attack from behind.

TAEGEUK IL JANG vs. TAEGEUK PAL JANG

Poom Exercise No. 33 (YANG)
Taegeuk Il Jang—Steps 5–8: Counter-attack with forward momentum (Heaven)

Push your arms apart to break his hold. Then turn left, using your body to obstruct his and smash your left hammer-fist into his groin. Punch his ribs with your right fist and unbalance the opponent by yanking him to your right side. Smash your left elbow down on his spine and finish him with a powerful punch to the kidneys.

POOM EXERCISE NO. 34 (UM/YIN)

Taegeuk Pal Jang—Steps 12–14: Counter-attack opponent while retreating (Earth)

Break free and spin around behind the opponent, twisting his left arm behind his back and apply an arm-bar. Use your right hand to push his immobilized left hand up his back to damage his shoulder. Smash your kick into his head and step backward, dragging him along by the left arm. Press your right hand against his elbow to apply an arm bar and force him down on his left knee. Step closer to his side and swing his left arm behind him, applying both wrist and elbow locks. Drop him to the ground with a head kick and jerk your right hand hard to break his wrist joint. Step back and push your left palm against his arm, dropping your weight on his elbow to break it.

PALGWE IL JANG vs. PALGWE PAL JANG

Poom Exercise No. 35 (YANG)

Palgwe Il Jang—Steps 13–16: Defeat the opponent with strikes while standing (Heaven)

Break free and step behind him on his right side, smashing your left fist into his groin. Strike his neck with your right knife-hand, forcing him backward. Strike his neck again with your left knife-hand. End the fight with a powerful blow to the solar plexus.

POOM EXERCISE NO. 36 (UM/YIN)
Palgwe Pal Jang—Steps 28–35: Defeat the opponent with strikes on the ground (Earth)

Against a second opponent's bear hug from behind, push your elbows out to break his hold and spin around to face him . Spread your arms against his arms thrusting them to either side before smashing into his lower ribs with twin uppercut punches. Then seize his right hand and strike his biceps with your knife-hand. Spin forward through a half-circle and thrust your elbow backwards to smash his ribs .Take him down with a hip wheel throw. End the fight on the ground with head strikes.

NOTES

_____

_____

_____

_____

_____

_____

_____

_____

_____

_____

_____

TAEGEUK EE JANG vs. TAEGEUK CHIL JANG

Poom Exercise No. 37 (YANG)

Taegeuk Ee Jang—Steps 5–8: Knock the opponent away with powerful strikes (Lake)

Break free and slip around him on your left side. Smash your right hammer-fist into his head. Then step forward and smash your left elbow into his spine as he folds up. Twist to the left, shoving him forwards in the same direction. Finish him with a kick and a punch to his head.

POOM EXERCISE NO. 38 (UM/YIN)

Taegeuk Chil Jang—Steps 5–8: Sweep the opponent to the ground and immobilize him (Mountain)

Break free and slip around him from your left side, scooping his left leg in your right hand. Sweep him off his feet and force his shoulder down with your left palm in a takedown. Mount his back and strike his neck with your right knife-hand. Push your left knee to arch his spine and hook your left forearm under his throat. Slap his ear hard with your right palm. Then seize his hair in your right fist and wrench it violently from his scalp. Alternatively, cup his chin in your palm and twist to break his neck.

PALGWE EE JANG vs. PALGWE CHIL JANG

Poom Exercise No. 39 (YANG)

Palgwe Ee Jang—Steps 13–16: Force open opponent's weak spot to exploit it (Lake)

Break free and turn left to face him. Pull his right arm and smash your left fist into his jaw. Wrench his right arm clockwise to damage his elbow . Push your left elbow against the back of his injured arm and crank it outwards to break his elbow .

End the fight with a powerful punch into his exposed left armpit.

POOM EXERCISE NO. 40 (UM/YIN)

Palgwe Chil Jang—Steps 15–23: Be still until opponent unwittingly exposes weak spot (Mountain)

Throw the first opponent on the ground obstructing the path of his friend who wields a club.

Block the attack from the second opponent and disarm him before punching his face. Swing through a half-circle dropping your weight down on the first man's body and knock him out by smashing your right fist down on his head.

Spin around to attack the second man's eyes and smash his face with your crescent kick. Push your forearm against his throat to apply a choke.

Break the rear bear hug from a third man by sliding sideways and pulling his arms apart. Step behind him, twisting his right arm behind his back in a chicken wing shoulder lock. Push his arm higher up his back to damage his shoulder.

TAEGEUK SAM JANG vs. TAEGEUK YUK JANG

Poom Exercise No. 41 (YANG)

Taegeuk Yuk Jang—Steps 5–7: Evade opponent and strike from the outside (Water)

Twist to the left, slipping around him like a snake squiggling through grass. Strike his neck with your right knife-hand and force down his head with your palm. Drop him with a knee strike to the jaw and lift his arm to expose his side . Strike a vital point deep inside his armpit. Finish him off with another kick and strike.

POOM EXERCISE NO. 42 (UM/YIN)
Taegeuk Sam Jang—Steps 5–8: Penetrate defense on the inside and adhere to opponent (Fire)

Break free and slip around him on your left side to strike his neck with your right knife-hand. Then push him backward and strike his neck again with your left knife-hand. Apply a wrist lock and swing your knife-hand into his armpit. Spin ninety degrees to your left, throwing him off-balance. Shift your weight forward and apply a chicken wing lock, pushing his arm up his back.

PALGWE SAM JANG vs. PALGWE YUK JANG

Poom Exercise No. 43 (YANG)

Palgwe Yuk Jang—Steps 14–19: Push opponent forward with strikes like a tidal wave (Water)

Break free and turn left to face him seizing his left arm and striking his biceps with your left knife-hand. Push his left arm upward with your left palm and smash his chest with your right palm-heel. Attack him with kicks and hand strikes to his knees, groin, chest, and head. Trap his left hand and strike his neck with your right knife-hand. Twist his left arm behind, spinning him around, and strike his head with your left knife-hand.

POOM EXERCISE NO. 44 (UM/YIN)
Palgwe Sam Jang—Steps 13–18: Withdraw to unbalance opponent and apply joint locks (Fire)

Break free by cranking your left hand to one side, then fling your right hand outward. Turn around through 180 degrees and slip past his left side. Unbalance him by pulling his right arm forwards and smash your left fist into his head.Step back again pulling him forwards and strike his head with your right fist. Apply an arm bar with your left forearm to the back of his right arm, forcing him to bend forwards. Step back again using your right hand to twist his hand behind in a shoulder lock. With your left forearm pushing against his shoulder, force him down on his chest. Twist sharply to your right, cranking his left wrist to damage his joint .

NOTES

_____

_____

_____

_____

_____

_____

_____

_____

_____

_____

_____

_____

_____

TAEGEUK SAH JANG vs. TAEGEUK OH JANG

Poom Exercise No. 45 (YANG)

Taegeuk Oh Jang—Steps 9 & 10: Knock opponent back with strikes (Wind)

Break free and twist around on your left side, striking his neck with your left knife-hand. Seize the opportunity to penetrate his defense and attack his face with your elbow. Capture his head inside your elbow and squeeze hard to choke him.

POOM EXERCISE NO. 46 (UM/YIN)

Taegeuk Sah Jang—Steps 9 & 10: Immobilize opponent and apply joint locks (Thunder)

Break free and twist around to seize his left hand with your right, twisting it clockwise. Push your left hand under his elbow to grab the back of his left shoulder and apply an arm bar. Kick his face and drop your weight, pushing on his wrist to break his elbow.

PALGWE SAH JANG vs. PALGWE OH JANG

Poom Exercise No. 47 (YANG)

Palgwe Oh Jang—Steps 24–27: Sweep opponent away with gale-force momentum (Wind)

Break free and turn left to face him. Sweep him off his feet with your left foot and hook your right elbow under his left arm to apply an arm bar. . Step forward, yanking up his left arm, and smash your right hammer-fist into his head. Step forwards again and smash your left fist down in his head. Knock him out with a strike to the jaw.

POOM EXERCISE NO. 48 (UM/YIN)

Palgwe Sah Jang—Steps 17–20: Shock opponent with abrupt directional change (Thunder)

Break free and turn left to face him. Force his left wrist behind him and strike his triceps with your left knife-hand. Thrust your knee upward into his chest and drop him on his knees. Subdue him with a chicken wing shoulder lock.

His friend suddenly seizes your outstretched hand, pulling you forward. Pull free by rotating your arm over your shoulder and swinging your left hammer-fist at his head. Finish the second opponent with a powerful strike to his solar plexus.

NOTES

_____

_____

_____

_____

_____

_____

_____

_____

_____

_____

_____

_____

_____

The Taegeuk and Palgwe poomsae add another dimension to self-defense with the incorporation of front or rear takedowns or hip and shoulder throws which inflict a devastating blow to the attacker from the hard impact with the ground. To ensure a successful throw in the "heat of battle" it is necessary to "soften up "the belligerent attacker by pummeling him into a state of reduced resistance, where he cannot counter an often less than perfect throwing technique.

Many sequences terminate with a kihap following the front low stance (ap kubi) and center punch(bandae montong jireugi).This may be recognized as inflicting a powerful stunning or distracting blow prior to the throw. To execute the throw, the defender advances around the opponent with a step to position his lead leg behind the attacker's legs and bumps the latter's hip. This body shove knocks the attacker off balance and makes it easier for the defender to control him by grabbing his lapels and turning his back to close the space between them. The defender straightens his knees and thrusts his hips upwards and backwards executing the hip throw by swinging through a 270 degrees turn sending the attacker air-borne over his hip to drop heavily on the ground. Similarly the defender can use a shoulder throw rather than the hip throw by flinging the attacker over his shoulders.

The patterns emphasize the versatility of different stances showing their importance to the defender's self-defense reaction. Aside for their obvious defensive appearance, they have a double edged nature and are easily wielded in counter-attacks...just like military transport is an essential part of logistics to a victorious mobile army. The speed of the offence may overwhelm the best defenses and throw the enemy's formations into confusion and complete rout .Forward advance means to capture and secure enemy territory. The same objective is demonstrated in Taekwondo poomsae.

The stances may be light and swift like using the front low stance to step past the opponent hooking your lead foot behind his for a backward sweep and rear takedown as you knock him to the floor...or the effort may be bold as you advance forwards to occupy his previous position with a long front stance after sending him reeling backwards by striking his vital points fiercely. Thus the stance is like a vehicle used to breach the enemy's defenses.

It may be heavy and static when used defensively in a horse back stance to counter a waist grab , bear hug or attempted throw…or a back stance useful in narrow confines when the defender can lean away to avoid the enemy's blows, or destabilize his balance by pulling his centre of gravity forwards ahead of his lead foot, combined with a sharp sweep of his front leg to knock him down.

An advantageous position is easily created when the defender uses the horse-back stance or back stance or crane stance to straddle the opponent's back crushing him under his weight in preparation to a rear choke or strike to the unguarded back of his head.

A quick defensive entry is afforded by a simple step forwards as in the walking stance…this is a very versatile stance natural to every man, woman or child who has learned to walk. In Taekwondo self-defense, the uniqueness of this upright stance is not merely in the ability to square-off and exchange blow for blow with the adversary, but to remain above him while raining heavy blows on vital points on his head and body from above. Strikes are less effective when thrown upwards from a crouch.

The cat or tiger stance is named after that ferocious animal, but its application uses wile and guile rather than raw brute strength of its animal counterpart. The defender can prevent the attacker's escape by stepping on the opponent's foot pinning it to the ground. Once immobilized, he is now very vulnerable to the defender's strikes aimed at his vital points.

The Taegeuk and Palgwe poomsae series can be used as a fountain of knowledge of different fighting tactics and strategies. Each attack from an opponent is a problem that demands a particular response which may only be suitable at that point in time depending on the unique circumstances of that environment. Thus the Taekwondo student is trained to be versatile and adaptable in deploying fight tactics according to the opponent's perceived strengths and weaknesses.

Fight strategies may be either Yang or Yin or combinations of both. Pure Yang techniques are solid and offensive, involving hard and ferocious strikes in an upright posture combined with forward momentum to knock the opponent backward with hard strikes. On the other hand are Yin or earth tactics that are soft and yielding, to manipulate the opponent's power against him by upsetting his balance and drawing him into your strike, or adhering close to opponent to apply defensive joint locks or throws. It may involve counter-attacks while retreating from an opponent or defeating the opponent with strikes on the ground.

The "Lake" strategy is manifested as inner firmness and outer softness, using Yang tactics like forcefully opening the opponent's weak spot to exploit it, flowing with aggressive forward momentum to overcome the opponent or knock him away with powerful strikes. It also borrows Yin tactics, like sinking your weight to break an opponent's grip or striking to immobilize an opponent in preparation for takedowns.

Next is the "Fire" stage, which encourages a sense of justice and ardor for training. This uses Yang tactics like direct strikes to break his defenses, focusing hard unyielding strikes at opponent's head to destabilize him, or seizing the opponent and counter-attacking with neck chops. It employs subtle Yin tactics to penetrate the opponent's defense on the inside and adhere to him, or withdrawal to unbalance opponent and apply joint locks.

The "Thunder," which is synonymous with great new-found power and dignity, is the third strategy. It relies on Yin tactics like sticking to an opponent and knocking him out with powerful strikes, immobilizing him to apply joint locks, drawing an opponent into hard strikes, or utilizing abrupt changes in direction to shock and overcome the opponent. It borrows Yang tactics which mainly push forcefully through the opponent's defenses.

The "Wind" strategy follows where the student learns how to respond with strength or weakness as the occasion demands. Yang techniques are applied to forcefully penetrate an opponent's core like a gale-force wind, rolling him back with cutting strikes. It also borrows Yin tactics to sweep the opponent off his feet like a whirlwind and knock him to the ground.

The "Water" strategy as the next important attribute demonstrates how the student must show mental flexibility with an incessant flow and softness rather than stagnation to overcome all obstacles. It applies defensive Yin techniques to stick to an opponent, flowing with an opponent's energy, drawing him down to be defeated on the ground, evading and avoiding direct confrontation to counter-strike from outside the opponent's reach. It borrows Yang tactics using hard strikes to "soften" the opponent up and overwhelm his resistance before applying joint locks or forcing an opponent forward with powerful strikes like a tidal wave.

The student should stand as strong and as firm as the "Mountain," enduring great physical and mental obstacles .This strategy uses Yin tactics, like being still and patient until the opponent unwittingly exposes his weak spot, controlling the opponent on the spot using stable stances to sweep, or clinch and force him to a submission hold on the ground. It borrows Yang tactics in the form of aggressive, full power open palm strikes.

CHAPTER 6

Taoist Ki Energy Theory

Once the student has performed the various Taegeuk and Palgwe poomsae several times, he or she should be able to achieve mastery of its various movements in terms of balance, agility, power development, concentration, and focus. It has been said that to be able to begin to master a particular form, one should have practiced it at least a thousand times. This refers to the external or Waegong aspects of poomsae training. Many students are stuck with a lifetime of training in these methods only to be able to emphasize the practical utility of poomsae techniques for self-defense or flamboyant or florid pleasing aesthetics.

There is another benefit to forms training which involves improving the student's overall health and even prolonging life. This focuses on the development of internal energy or Naegong, where the movements may be performed at a slower speed with supple body motions, and with special slow breathing methods while maintaining a serene or calm mind. Indeed, the aphorism of performing at least a thousand repetitions of each form is even more applicable here in order to develop these internal energies. Thus Taekwondo training requires a lifetime of practice to appreciate the esoteric details incorporated within its forms. The practitioner should have a clear understanding and decide before each practice whether the performance will be based on the Waegong or the Naegong method.

The Naegong practice aims to develop ki or internal energy. At this point many students may wonder: What is ki? Why is it important to my Taekwondo training? How do I know it is real?

According to Oriental philosophy that originated in India or China many centuries ago, ki is the universal cosmic energy that surrounds and permeates every living being and non-living object. This basic concept has been developed further into profound philosophical teachings that have influenced different cultures, religions like Hinduism and Buddhism, and martial arts, including Taekwondo.

Taekwondo is sometimes described as a way of life with the aim of developing the individual physically, emotionally, and spiritually into a whole person. The "do" in Taekwondo refers to the unique philosophy of the Tao that underpins this unique martial art without which its many techniques may be nothing more than mere physical exercises or dance choreography. The development of ki energy within the practitioner is the ultimate aim of Taekwondo training. According to martial arts theory and teaching, this is also associated with improved health and longevity.

ANCIENT TAOIST WORLD VIEWS ON KI ENERGY

Chinese traditional medicine believes that there are two types of ki within each person. The first one is the prenatal ki which we acquire from both parents at the time of conception, and the other, the postnatal ki, flows into us through breathing, eating, and drinking as well as exercise. The prenatal ki is of limited supply and once depleted, the essence of your life-force is gone.

Taekwondo training aims to develop the postnatal ki in order to increase it and improve its flow as well as achieving the internal balance to maintain excellent health.

Lao Tzu wrote in the Tao Te Ching:

The tao that can be told
is not the eternal Tao.
The name that can be named
is not the eternal Name...
The Tao is called the Great Mother:
empty yet inexhaustible,
it gives birth to infinite worlds.
It is always present within you.
You can use it any way you want...

Traditionally, Asian philosophers have identified seven energy centers in the body which some believe may correspond to the major nerve plexuses or junctions located in the body's midline. These are said to include the crown energy center just above the top of the head, the upper danjun inside the brain in the region of the limbic system, the pharyngeal plexus in the throat, the cardiac plexus around the heart, the solar plexus in the upper abdomen or stomach area, the hypogastric plexus or lower danjun just below the umbilicus, and the sacral plexus or root energy center located at the most distal part of the spine. Ki energy is thought to circulate into and reside within these rich nerve junctions and centers. The two most important ki storage areas are the lower danjun, the root energy center in the pelvis, as well as inside the bone marrow. It is not without reason or foundation that many training camps forbid boxers from engaging in any sexual intercourse for up to three months before a championship fight. Flouting of this rule may lead to the dissipation of the fighter's ki energy, resulting in a raw, empty feeling inside the marrow and a mental and physical sluggishness causing him to lose his fight.

Another example is the mental confusion in an epileptic that may last for hours or days following the wholesale electrical discharge of brain cells or epileptic fit before an eventual full recovery. Even Christianity has an example of this energy dissipation. The Christian Bible reads in Luke 8:43-48, "[43]And a woman having an issue of blood twelve years, which had spent all her living upon physicians, neither could be healed of any. [44]Came behind him, and touched the border of his garments: and immediately her issue of blood stanched. [45]And Jesus said, Who touched me? When all denied, Peter and they that were with him said, Master, the multitude throng thee and press thee, and sayest thou, Who touched me? [46]And Jesus said, Somebody hath touched me: for I perceive that virtue is gone out of me. [47]And when the woman saw that she was not hid, she came trembling, and falling down before him, she declared unto him before all the people for what cause she had touched him, and how she was healed immediately. [48]And he said unto her, Daughter, be of good comfort: thy faith hath made thee whole, go in peace..."

SOURCE OF KI ENERGY

The source of everything is explained by the Tao, or universal law, according to Chinese philosophy. The Korean cosmology is similar and refers to this universal law as the Taegeuk. The world exists as one entity comprised of two opposite and complementary forces: Yang, or positive energy, and Yin, or negative energy.

The interaction between these two forces creates the third force, which is ki, the immaterial breath found in everything. The Taoists believe that the source of the ki energy on Earth is the North Star Polaris and the constellation of the Big Dipper, which radiate both forms of the ki energies throughout the galaxy, which includes our universe and solar system. This cosmic force holds together the earth, the solar system, and all the other stars, and radiates cosmic particles down on every creature. Humans are said to be able to absorb this cosmic particle force through the crown, the Third Eye spot, and in the air we breathe, utilizing it to sustain our soul, spirit, and organs. After death, the spirits of the enlightened ones are transformed and transported back to their stellar origins, passing through the North Star to get to Heaven.

Other world views have identified the Sirius star system as the source of all energy in our universe. This is comprised of Sirius A, a star twice as large as our sun with more than twenty-five times its brightness, and Sirius B, an ancient green dwarf star that has completed its life cycle and has condensed to an Earth-like size, transforming its gaseous hydrogen plasma to ionized hydrogen crystal after ejecting its outer atmosphere.

Sirius B is the oldest, smallest, and densest of celestial objects, and by spinning fast it draws the hydrogen essence from the younger Sirius A and ejects it as a stream through the universe. Its ionic energy is piezo-electric, which is a rapidly pulsating mechanical action created by the immense gravitational pressure within the dense core of the star generating electrical current. Piezo-electric crystals can expand and contract rapidly after stimulation by electricity; turning rapidly pulsing electrical currents into rapidly pulsing mechanical action, and conversely generating electricity when distorted mechanically. This ionized hydrogen light stream from Sirius B resonates on Earth at a frequency of seven to twelve hertz or cycles per second, similar to the brain's alpha wave frequency induced during relaxation and meditation.

In man, ki manifests as five different aspects of energy or the five elements—Fire, Earth, Metal, Water, and Wood. Nature exists in these different energy forms, each a blend of Yang and Yin. Human beings are thought to be made up of a balance of these five elements. The essence of the Taegeuk is to keep us in fine balance, as a healthy body usually means a healthy mind and spirit.

Divergent Asian cultures recognize ki as the life-giving heavenly energy made manifest through the breath and every living creature—human, animal, and plant—is thought to possess a bio-electric aura. In order words, no breath means no life. This aura is further described as a supernatural force of life within each person more akin to an invisible ether that links up with a greater and more diffuse external ether bathing and surrounding us. This ether is thought to exist in the air we breathe, the food we eat, in our drink, and can also be obtained through exercise.

At present, no human instruments can directly record or measure the existence of this force. However, old paintings of saints usually acknowledge this aura, depicting it with the bright circular haloes that radiate from their heads. The subliminal message here is that one has to attain a higher religious level and training to cultivate this cosmic energy with the aura blossoming like a flowering plant, showing luxuriant growth after exposure to strong sunlight.

TAOIST THEORIES OF ENERGY FLOW

How do you draw ki energy inside the body?

This is achieved by utilizing deep rhythmic abdominal breathing as a pump to pull fresh air into the lungs and activate the emotional limbic system and diaphragm.

According to Taoist philosophy, breathing is the primary way we bring energy into the body. Once inside our bodies, we extract energy from the inspired breath and store it in the lower abdomen or danjun. The more we can extract and store, the better our physical condition becomes.

Taekwondo poomsae reveal the steps that are involved in ki energy channeling. These methods are concealed in the different jumbi seogi techniques performed at the beginning and ending of each pattern.

The reversed abdominal breathing technique is used in these steps to maximize energy creation. One should stand relaxed but alert with both feet placed shoulder width apart for balance. The center of gravity should be lowered and the pelvic bone tucked in. In this position, the chin should be also be tucked in with the eyes looking ahead, while the mind focuses its attention on the danjun.

Visualize a concentric shape of the eight-sided octagonal diagram of the Palgwe drawn around the center of your abdomen with an outer diameter of about six inches. It should enclose a smaller four-inch diameter octagon, which in turn encloses an even smaller two-inch sized octagon with its center at your navel. When inhaling slowly, the hands should be made to trace along the outermost border of the Palgwe diagram from below, rising to the top, which is at the solar plexus. The mind should be focused on spiralling the ki energy several times anti-clockwise as the hands rise. Then the hands are closed into fists and pushed down to the lowest level of the diagram at a level opposite the danjun exhaling, only two-thirds of the expired air before stopping the breath. This second phase also uses the mind to spiral the ki energy in a reverse direction into progressively smaller circles at the navel before channeling it into the danjun for storage. The proper method involves slow exhalation, avoiding excessive muscular tension and continually using the mind to direct the energy down through the middle of the body to the lower abdomen, as though both compressing a spring and simultaneously pushing it down into the danjun.

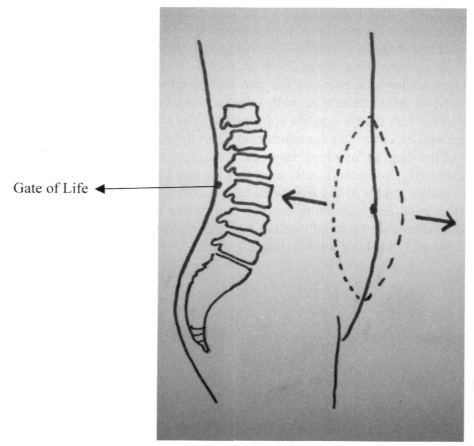

Gate of Life ◄───────────

PICTURE 4
Gate of Life Pressure Point in Lower Spine

The energy breathing methods are also seen in the slow dynamic muscular contraction steps found in the Taegeuk poomsae and black belt poomsae. Patterns may be practiced with health and mental benefits in mind through ki development and circulation. This is exemplified more succinctly through the early introduction of ki training within the Taegeuk poomsae rather than the older Palgwe set, where such studies were reserved for those that attained the black belt level.

Taegeuk Yuk Jang develops more advanced reverse abdominal breathing techniques to circulate the ki energy within the body. In Step 10, the position of the lower back is made part of the deep breathing exercise while the mind is focused on the danjun, and the chest remains relaxed. Taoist theory mandates that the abdomen and lower back should contract into each other when inhaling, and push apart while exhaling, stimulating a very important acupuncture point on the lower spine called the "Gate of Life," as well as the kidneys, to energize the entire body's vitality.

Paradoxically, Taegeuk Pal Jang, the last of the eight patterns before the black belt promotion test, may also be considered the beginning of a new understanding of the Taegeuk poomsae series. It symbolizes the Earth with its meaning of the root and settlement, and also the beginning of everything. This is exemplified in Steps 5–8, which are performed at slow speed and simulates the pulling up of vast ki energy reserve into the body from the earth below.

In koryo poomsae, the junbi seogi is the Tong milgi, which involves visualizing an energy ball located within the danjun. Focus your mind as you lift the imaginary energy ball upward, absorbing more energy from the upper abdominal energy center and projecting it into your empty hands.

For Pyongwon, Cheonkwon, and Hansu poomsae, the junbi seogi is the Kyopson junbi seogi utilizing overlapping hands in front of the groin to concentrate ki energy in the sacral plexus or root energy center. The mental imagery involves forcing the ki down into the lowest of the seven energy centers of the body using both open palms.

Finally, Taegeuk Chil Jang and Ilyeo poomsae demonstrate the Bo jumeok Moa seogi or covered fist closed stance where the Taekwondo practitioner draws ki energy upward through the body from the feet rooted in the ground. The Taoist philosophy believes that ki energy in the body naturally moves upward. When the ki in the body is raised, it is very easy to perform aerial techniques. However, if the ki in the body is high, a person will also feel restless like a tiger in a cage—a very dangerous creature to encounter when released.

Healing breath to maintain balance and harmony.
…Breathe on me, Breath of the Divine,
Fill me with life anew,
That I may love what thou dost love,
And do what thou wouldst do.
Breathe on me, Breath of the Divine,
Until my heart is pure,
Until with thee I will one will,
To do and to endure.
Breathe on me, Breath of the Divine,
Till I am wholly thine,
Till all this earthly part of me,
Glows with thy face divine…

Without breath, there can be no life. Cessation of oxygen transport to the brain usually leads to death within five minutes. Similarly, when ki energy has left the body completely death immediately follows. No other substances are of such profound necessity to us.

From the Tao Te Ching:

…The Tao begets the one,
The one begets the two
The two beget the three and
The three beget the ten thousand things.
All things are backed by the shade,
Faced by the light
And harmonized by the immaterial breath.

How does ki energy flow within the body?

Chinese traditional medicine identifies twelve channels through which ki energy flows. The front of the body contains the Yin channels which lead the ki energy downward from the lips to the groin, and these are namely the lung, the spleen, the heart, the kidney, the pericardium, and the liver meridians. They are named after the solid organs in the body and connect with these organs internally and the limbs externally.

The Yang channels are named after the hollow organs and include the large intestine, the stomach, the small intestine, the bladder, the triple heater, and the gall bladder meridians. They enable the ki energy to flow upward along the back toward the head. Through each of these meridians the ki energy is said to flow to the next one, completing a cycle every twenty-four hours.

There are eight other vessels which connect to the meridians but lack a direct connection to the internal organs. The most important of these include the two midline channels, the first of which is called the Conception Vessel. It begins at the perineum, extending up the front of the body to the face. Its counterpart, the Governing Vessel, also starts from the perineum but rises up the back and over the back of the head to end at the philtrum. These two vessels make a complete energy circuit when the tip of the tongue touches the roof of the mouth, an important aspect of meditation.

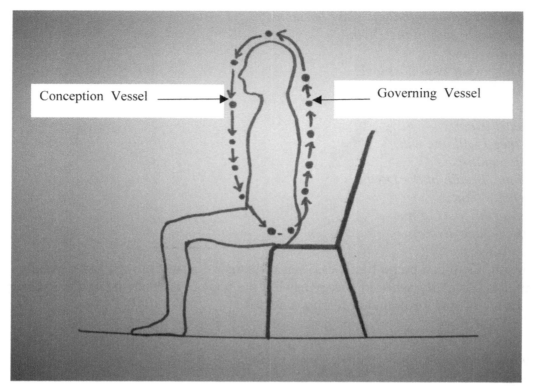

PICTURE 5
Midline Ki Channels: Conception Vessel and Governing Vessel

Ki energy is manifested in the different organs and meridians of the body in each of the five aspects. Ancient Taoist teachings describe the following twenty-four hour rhythm of ki energy circulating within the twelve meridians of the body:

Large Intestine (Metal/Yang energy):	5–7 a.m.
Stomach (Earth/Yang energy):	7–9 a.m.
Spleen (Earth/Yin energy):	9–11 a.m.
Heart (Fire/Yin energy):	11 a.m.–1 p.m.
Small Intestine (Fire/Yang energy):	1–3 p.m.
Bladder (Water/Yang energy):	3–5 p.m.
Kidneys (Water/Yin energy):	5–7 p.m.
Pericardium (Fire/Yin energy):	7–9 p.m.
Triple Heater (Fire/Yang energy):	9–11 p.m.
Gall Bladder (Wood/Yang energy):	11p.m.–1 a.m.
Liver (Wood/Yin energy):	1–3 a.m.
Lungs (Metal/Yin energy):	3–5 a.m.

The Yang meridians representing the hollow organs are concerned with the functions of digestion of nutrients and elimination of waste, while the Yin meridians which represent solid organs deal with the function of circulation of blood and other bodily fluids.

Fire energy in its Yang form circulates within the small intestine and the triple heater meridians, and while in Yin form, the heart and the pericardium meridians. Fire is hot and bright, and in its strong form it includes traits like decisiveness, confidence, and charisma. When it is weak, it manifests with anxiety, restlessness, and hypertension.

Earth energy in Yang form is identified with the stomach meridian, and in Yin form with the spleen meridian. Its strengths include self-discipline, responsibility, and reliability. When Earth energy is deficient, digestive problems are common, as well as a lack of clear thinking.

For Metal energy, the Yang form concentrates within the large intestine meridian, and the lung meridian in Yin form respectively. When abundant, it represents determination, self-reliance, and energy, and its deficiency is manifest as breathing problems, colds, and constipation.

Wood energy manifests in Yang form in the gall bladder meridian and the liver meridian in the Yin form respectively. Strong Wood energy manifests as systematic thinking, inner confidence, and optimism. In its deficiency, it is associated with anger and indecisiveness.

Water energy in its Yang form represents the energy flow within the bladder meridian, and in Yin form, the kidney meridian. Its strengths include fearlessness and perseverance through willpower. Its deficiency is manifest in fearful and withdrawal states, urination difficulties, as well as fertility problems.

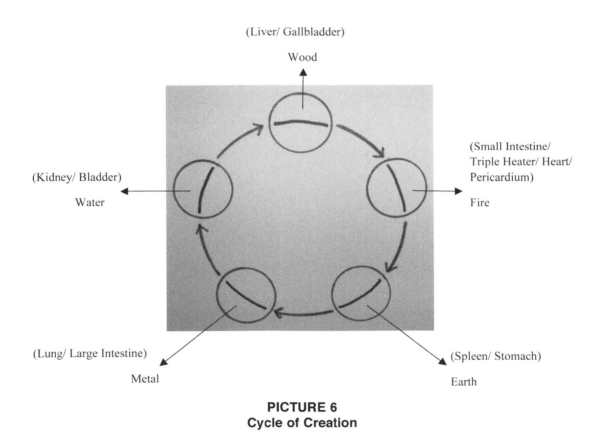

PICTURE 6
Cycle of Creation

Ki is believed to flow in two cycles which either enhance or dissipate the energy level. The first one is referred to as the Cycle of Creation, as shown above, where the ki flows from the large intestine meridian in turn through the meridians of the stomach, spleen, heart, small intestine, bladder, kidneys, pericardium, triple heater, gall bladder, liver, lungs, and back again to the large intestine meridian to start another twenty-four hour cycle. The ki level at each meridian can be increased by striking a vital point on the preceding meridian at an appropriate angle based on the normal direction of energy flow. Changing the angle of the strike may cause stagnation or even reversal of ki flow, short-circuiting the system and leading to an over-abundance of Yang or Yin energy.

- Fire to Wood (from any of the meridians of the pericardium, triple heater, heart, or small intestine to the liver or gall bladder).
- Wood to Water (from the meridians of the liver or gall bladder to the kidneys or bladder).
- Water to Metal (from the meridians of the kidneys or bladder to the lungs or large intestine).
- Metal to Earth (from the meridians of the lungs or large intestine to the spleen or stomach).
- Earth to Fire (from the meridians of the spleen or stomach to the pericardium, triple heater, heart, or small intestine).

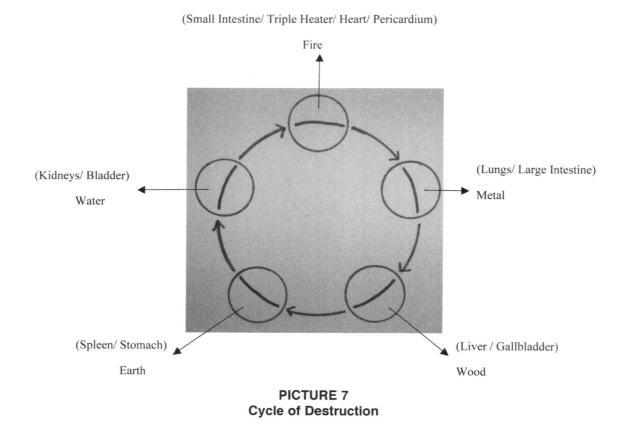

PICTURE 7
Cycle of Destruction

The other pathway is the Cycle of Destruction, where the ki levels are dissipated through sequential striking of a point on each meridian. In this case, the ki is destroyed by striking the five elements in any of the following sequences:

- Fire to Metal (striking any of the meridians of the pericardium, triple heater, heart, or small intestine, followed by the lungs or large intestine).
- Metal to Wood (striking the meridians of the lungs or large intestine followed by the liver or gall bladder).

- Wood to Earth (striking the meridians of the liver or gall bladder followed by the spleen or stomach).
- Earth to Water (striking the meridians of the spleen or stomach followed by the kidneys or bladder).
- Water to Fire (striking the meridians of the kidneys or bladder followed by any of the pericardium, triple heater, heart, or small intestine).

There are different ways of manipulating the vital points of the body in the martial arts and these are generally referred to as Hoshinbup (self-defense methods), Salbup (killing methods), and Hwalbup (resuscitation methods). They are further separated into five strategies which include attacking pressure points along a meridian, taking advantage of vulnerability in the diurnal cycle, attacking Yin and Yang weak points in sequence, strikes to special ki gates or points, and skillful utilization of the cycles of creation and destruction.

The major difference between Taekwondo, Karate, and Kung Fu lies in the emphasis each art puts on the preferred method of vital point strikes. The first two attack methods are not emphasized in Taekwondo, unlike the other martial arts. Instead, its focus lies in the manipulation of the last three methods.

The Yin and Yang methods incorporate sequential attacks to each point or meridian, or to the left and right sides, or above and below the waist, or front and back. The cycles of creation and destruction present special points which, when used in proper sequence, can create excess Yang or excess Yin states in the body. Care should be taken when manipulating these points, as a three point strike can easily cause a knockout, while a five point hit is dangerous and can even cause death. In our present world, it is almost always unnecessary to take another's life even in the face of great provocation. It is important that the martial artist refrain from undertaking this irreversible action except in the gravest of situations that threaten his or her life, or those of their loved ones.

How do you get ki energy to flow smoothly?

Taekwondo training and particularly poomsae practice enjoins the practitioner to tread softly but carry a big stick. This metaphor hearkens back to the Taekwondo's Taoist roots manifested as smooth, soft, circular movements to enhance the relaxation of the underlying muscles. At the start of a technique, taking in a breath while uncoiling the body assists in the relaxation of the muscles to conserve energy. Releasing the expired air by contracting the lungs and the body forcefully at the end of the movement leads to energy concentration.

Taekwondo techniques are faster and more powerful when there is little tension in the muscles with active muscular contraction, focus, and power generation being applied only at the last stage of the movement. Heavy muscle tension means slower speed and easy fatigability, and in turn this results in striking techniques that generate less power.

Tension in the muscles also causes stagnation of ki energy. This is manifest as a decrease in the electrical resistance in the skin at that point with the static energy leading to a leakage of ki. This is indirectly witnessed during moments of increased mental stress and muscular tension where electrical static is observed as a discharge from the fingertips upon contact with a metallic object, only to disappear by focusing on deep relaxation and rhythmic breathing.

Trying hard involves effort, which in turn creates tension which blocks energy flow with less power generated. Energy is easily obstructed in areas of tension and thus is prevented from reaching the reservoir in the lower abdomen. Ultimately, these blockages in the energy pathways lead to organ dysfunction. The Taekwondo student needs to be relaxed in movement in order to let go of tension. By invoking muscular relaxation to remove all the blocks to ki circulation, the circulation of bio-electric energy through the meridians can be enhanced.

NOTES

CHAPTER 7

MODERN VIEWS ON KI ENERGY

How do I know that ki energy exists?

The best test of the importance of any object or matter is when it is missing or absent. How do you know how important a loved one is? Deep aching of the heart always occurs with the prolonged separation from loved ones. In the event of the death of a loved one, this is usually associated with a period of mourning associated with a painful sadness and a feeling of profound emptiness.

How important is water to you? Imagine you are stranded somewhere in the middle of the desert and your throat is dry and parched, having drank the last drops from your water bottle two days earlier. Every mirage on the horizon appears to take the form of an oasis of cool drinking water. Water has never tasted sweeter when you finally stumble on a cool oasis.

You start to feel light-headed and your last meal was more than twelve hours earlier. You are feeling hungry and your blood sugar level must have plummeted. Eating a quick meal rapidly relieves the abdominal pangs and light-headedness.

Ki energy can be subjected to similar tests by inducing an absence in order to prove its existence.

This can be demonstrated in the following mundane, everyday examples:

You wake up in the morning still groggy from being sleep-deprived. Then you drag yourself to the wash basin in your bathroom and splash some water on your face. Instantly your consciousness clears up and you are wide awake.

That didn't work? Then try this.

Take a quick shower, trying to shake the cobwebs out of your sleepy head. After the bath, a vigorous rub across your mid- and lower-back as you dry yourself with a towel never fails to send a flood of awakening energy and alertness up your back to your brain.

You are having a lazy, dozy afternoon having exhausted yourself that morning cleaning your home. You seem to have forgotten all about an important appointment as your body sinks into the comfort of your living room cushions. Every minute on the sofa seems to sap your will to stay awake, just like the pet cat sleeping on the rug a foot away.

An eternity later, the cat suddenly comes awake and twitches its ear to a vague rodent scratching noise from the garden outside. Its hunting instinct comes to the fore as it stretches its spine taut and bares its fangs in a silent feline yawn before slinking off out of sight to its new adventure.

That is the impetus you need as you suddenly remember your appointment. You jump off of the sofa and stretch, imitating your cat even without thinking. Fingers lock together above your head as you arch your back. You pause, standing on tiptoes, and pull all your spinal nerves and muscles tight. Your body becomes energized, as if an on/off switch was suddenly activated.

There are many more examples which each one of us can think of from our daily experiences.

BREATH WORK

Ki energy is also cultivated in Taekwondo by using the breathing exercises in poomsae as a vehicle of active meditation. Yet the concept may be simpler in the theory than in practice. A simple breathing exercise involves smelling the air, concentrating its pristine currents around the roof of your nasal cavities just like animals sniff the air for the slightest whiff of a predator's scent. It is a survival technique which we have all but forgotten in our modern and safe world free from the terrors of an attack from wild beasts.

The importance of our nose is easily overlooked in this breathing process. The scent of fear or death linking with primal survival instincts is well known to energize a desperate animal to seek escape from predators. In humans, various scents may bring on feelings of revulsion or pleasure, which is innate or based on our experiences. Our subconscious mind is said to be able to recognize the smell of fear that emanates from potential attackers. This may enable us to read the excited attacker's intent and withdraw from that dangerous environment, reducing the possibility of an imminent attack. The field of aromatherapy is a vocation that exploits the use of pleasant scents of various soothing oils to induce a state of relaxation and well-being.

The sequence of events starts as soon as scent molecules hit the chemoreceptors of the olfactory nerves located in the roof of our nasal cavities. These are the only nerves in the body that are directly exposed to the outside world. Once stimulated, they convey electrical currents speedily to the limbic cortex of the brain, which serves to coordinate our emotions, motivation, autonomic nerves, and hormonal functions, which are not under the direct control of our conscious mind.

Fear energy can be manipulated in the amygdale, a part of the limbic cortex, by meditation to achieve a state of no thought or *mushim*. Anticipation of the fear of pain is often the primary cause of defeat in a fight. Also, strong unpleasant smells like those from the release of bowel contents, blood, or fear trigger strong emotional and subconscious messages that can undermine the will to fight for survival. Drugged or mentally ill people may experience no fear of pain and so are very dangerous to fight against. Meditative breathing by inducing a state of mushim helps to modulate the fear of pain through stimulation of the limbic cortex.

Through the myriad neural connections, bio-electric energy can be transmitted downward from the limbic system to recharge the splanchnic nerves which control the sympathetic and parasympathetic nervous systems. The splanchnic nerves are found in the major energy centers of the pharyngeal plexus, the cardiac plexus, the solar plexus, and the hypogastric plexus mentioned earlier, and influence the release of adrenaline from the nerve endings of the sympathetic nervous system, or acetyl-choline, a chemical from the nerves of the parasympathetic nervous system.

The splanchnic nerves in the solar plexus control the flow of blood to the stomach lining and also influence the balance and release of hormones and enzymes whose actions maintain the integrity of the digestive tract. An important sign of impending death in people who have suffered severe brain injury is the occurrence of spontaneous bleeding from the stomach. This is one example of the subconscious interactions between the nerve cells of the upper brain and the neurons of the peripheral nervous system.

Adrenaline serves the purpose of inducing the fight or flight response of the body to stressful situations by doubling the heart rate, which increases the flow of blood to the skeletal muscles in anticipation of sudden muscular exertion and may exacerbate anxiety by causing the uncomfortable forceful thumping of the heart within its thoracic cage, and increasing the respiratory rate (which improves the amount of oxygen available to the muscles but may paradoxically induce light-headedness from reduced blood flow to the brain). It reduces blood flow through the skin to reduce the severity of bleeding from any wounds inflicted, initially dilates the pupils to improve vision by increasing the availability of light to the retina, and later narrows the visual field, making peripheral vision next to impossible. It dries the secretions of the salivary glands, making audible and clear speech difficult, while making the muscles more excitable and twitchy with the eventual loss of fine motor skills and the retention of only gross motor action. The activity of the bowel is reduced by diverting its blood flow, and in extreme situations causes the sudden embarrassing release of the bowel contents or urine.

Constant activation of the adrenaline system eventually leads to a highly stressed person at great risk of heart disease, stroke, depression, and dementia.

The parasympathetic nervous system in simple terms does the opposite, soothing the body and calming the heart as it returns the body to its pre-excited state capable of planned thought and action. The essence of the meditating mind is to allow the parasympathetic state to dominate.

The intake of breath also draws the fresh ki in the air deep into the chest, causing a downward displacement of the diaphragm and massage of the abdominal organs as the lower abdomen is pushed out. This is said to result in stimulation of the solar plexus and pelvic plexus with resultant increase in the circulation of the internal bio-electric current or ki within these nerve centers and organs.

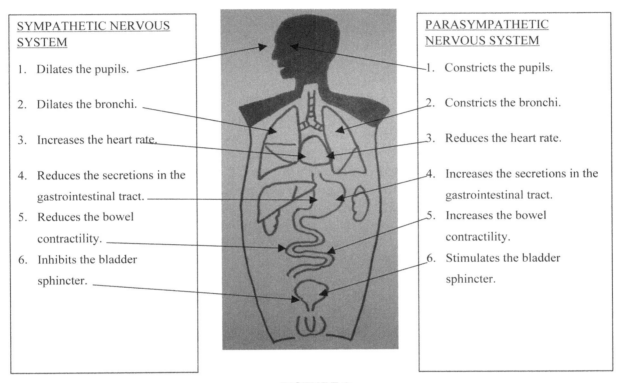

PICTURE 8
Sympathetic and Parasympathetic Nervous Systems

Poomsae training involves the use of two separate types of breathing techniques aiming to foster the circulation of the body's ki energy. The first is abdominal diaphragmatic breathing, which involves slowly filling and expanding the lungs with air while moving the diaphragm downward. This forces the lower abdomen to relax and bulge out during inspiration. Then the lower abdomen contracts in expiration, forcing the diaphragm upward. This technique helps to lower the blood pressure and slow the heart rate while increasing the elimination of toxins from the body.

In a physical conflict, it becomes a vital necessity for one to guard against a sudden strike to the torso during inspiration. Such a blow is likely to interrupt the downward flow of ki from the breath to the danjun, leading to its dispersal. In the event of that happening, one would easily be at the mercy of an adversary.

The second main technique is reversed abdominal breathing, which involves expanding the upper part of the lungs in inspiration while pulling in the lower belly, contracting the abdominal organs in the process.

When releasing the breath, the lower abdomen is pushed out in direct contrast to the first technique. This is helpful in circulating ki quickly around the body, generating a lot of power, and is primarily used in the jumbi seogi as well as techniques that emphasize slow dynamic tension and kihaps.

NEURO-ENDOCRINE BASIS OF KI ENERGY FLOW

The circulation of ki energy within the twelve meridians closely approximates the twenty-four-hour circadian cycle in humans which is based on a sleep-wake rhythm. Sleep is associated with the increased secretion of melatonin, a hormone produced in the pineal gland, while the wakeful state is characterized by the suppression of this hormone. This follows a light-dark cycle where daylight is absorbed through the retina and electrical impulses are transmitted to the suprachiasmatic nucleus (SCN) of the hypothalamus, which is the primary biological or circadian clock of the body. The SCN also sends signals to the pineal gland to influence the release of melatonin which in turn feeds back on the SCN to modify the rhythm of its circadian clock. In daylight and the awakened state, there is maximal suppression of melatonin secretion. At night or in the absence of light, there is peaking of melatonin secretion.

The SCN also interacts with the paraventricular nucleus and supraoptic nucleus, which are parts of the hypothalamus that serve as the primary coordination centers for the circadian release of the pituitary hormones and control of the autonomic nervous system. The pituitary gland is the master gland that controls the rest of the endocrine glands and in effect the entire metabolic state of the body. The main hormones released by the pituitary gland include adrenocorticotropic hormone (ACTH), which regulates the adrenal corticosteroid release; thyroid-stimulating hormone (TSH), which stimulates thyroid hormone production; growth hormone (GH), which stimulates the linear growth of the body and tissue repair; luteinizing hormone (LH) and follicle-stimulating hormone (FSH), which by stimulating the ovaries and testes regulate sexual maturity and fertility; anti-diuretic hormone (ADH), which stimulates the kidneys to prevent the excessive loss of the body's water; and prolactin and oxytocin, which stimulate the development of the breast and milk production in women as well as coordinate uterine contractions during childbirth.

Melatonin secretion starts to peak at 9 p.m. once it is no longer suppressed by the ambient daylight, and is followed by the increased secretion of the other hormones, with prolactin peaking at midnight, TSH peaking between 10 p.m. and 4 a.m., and GH peaking in the early hours of the morning correlating with rapid eye movement (REM) stage 3 and 4 sleep. Melatonin secretion stops at daybreak concurrently with the peak secretion of ACTH between 6 and 9 a.m. in the wakeful state, and the adrenal steroid cortisol reaches maximal levels at 8 a.m. There is evidence to show that LH and FSH release also peaks at the same time followed by peak testosterone levels at 9 a.m.

In the daytime, the major physiologic functions of the body are concerned with remaining alert with maximal cardiovascular efficiency and muscle strength, eating and digestion of food, and elimination of the bodily waste. These functions are also influenced by the peak secretion of other neuropeptides and neurohormones including dopamine, which helps maintain alertness, gamma amino butyric acid (GABA), which has a calming effect, serotonin, which helps with impulse control, and gastrin-releasing peptide (GIP), which influences the hunger signal along with neuropeptideY.

Ki energy flows within the large intestine meridian between 5 and 7 a.m., which stimulates this organ to receive and discharge waste, freeing up bowel space in anticipation of the coming meals. Between 7 and 9 a.m., the stomach meridian is coordinating the earth ki energy derived from the start of the process of digestion of food.

From 9 to 11 a.m., the spleen meridian receives and dispenses the energy derived from digestion. This may be a manifestation of the circadian rhythm of the spleen which is stimulated by the adrenal steroid cortisol and testosterone. Under the influence of these important metabolic hormones, the body's immune function is enhanced when the spleen increases the number of white blood cells (WBC) and red blood cells

(RBC) in circulation. Ki is sometimes described as the captain of blood; the secreted hormones act as forms of Yang ki able to influence the production of blood, which is Yin ki.

The heart meridian is active with Yin energy from 11 a.m. to 1 p.m., creating a fire to increase the overall circulation of blood transporting oxygen, the absorbed nutrients from the digested meal, and ki to the tissues for metabolism. Blood is described as the mother of ki; this underscores its important role in the transport of vital Yang ki in the form of nutrients, oxygen, hormones, and proteins to distant sites to nourish and fuel important metabolic processes. Upon its return to the heart it is able to ensure the cooling of the body by drawing away the heat of combustion generated from the active metabolism in the tissues. This heat is eliminated as sweat through the skin or in the expired breath.

Between 1 and 3 p.m., the small intestine meridian also circulates the fire ki derived from the Yang energy released once the food is broken down further into smaller bits. The bladder meridian acts as a conduit for Yang energy and receives and stores the waste water for excretion with the main ki flow occurring between 3 and 5 p.m. Yin ki flows in the kidney meridian between 5 and 7 p.m., enabling the kidneys to coordinate the gathering and dispensing of water throughout the body. This helps to maintain the body's hydration, temperature through conservation, or appropriate elimination of water. The highest body temperature and blood pressure usually occur between 6 and 7 p.m. More fire and Yin energy are present in the pericardium meridian between 7 and 9 p.m.

Between 9 and 11 p.m., as darkness falls, melatonin secretion starts and bowel movements are suppressed. This is also the time of activity in the triple heater meridian carrying the Yang energy which is generated from the activities of the "lower heater," which includes the intestines, the "middle heater," which processes the food in the stomach, and the "upper heater," which includes the lungs and the ki processed from the air.

The gall bladder meridian is active with Yang energy between 11p.m. and 1 a.m., when the gall bladder constitutes and stores the bile prior to later release to help the digestion of food. Between 1 and 3 a.m., Yin energy flows in the liver meridian, enabling the circadian function of the liver to store the excess blood that is not utilized in the low metabolic state during sleep. .

The lung meridian moves the vital Yin energy throughout the body between 3 and 5 a.m. This occurs during the deep refreshing sleep in REM stages 3 and 4 and allows the important repairs to the body's damaged tissues to take place. It also coincides with the temporary paralysis of the rest of the respiratory muscles, allowing only the diaphragm to act as the sole respiratory muscle. The deep descent of the diaphragm improves the oxygen intake and like a pump enhances the circulation of the major fluids within the body including the blood, the lymph, and the cerebro-spinal fluid.

The performance of Taekwondo poomsae requires the withdrawal of the practitioner into an isolated world where the controlling influences of our major senses are diminished. Thus there is less distraction from our sight and hearing as one flows through the steps of each poomsae.

SCIENTIFIC EVIDENCE OF KI CHANNELS

There is indirect evidence of the existence of these energy channels. One such is the numbing pain frequently felt in the inner part of the left elbow and the inner aspect of the left hand when someone suffers a heart attack. This follows the same distribution of the heart meridian identified by Chinese traditional medicine centuries ago.

Another example is the occasional constriction of the coronary arteries of the heart in susceptible people when their hands are exposed to cold temperatures despite the obvious lack of a proper direct channel. There is also the cardiac arrest that has occurred on rare occasion when a woman's cervix is handled with a metal clamping instrument prior to pelvic surgery, indicating the presence of hidden channel linking these disparate organs.

ENERGY RELAY POINTS

Clapping the hands and tapping the feet are universally associated with a higher level of ecstasy when listening to music in different cultures. Located at the center of the palm and foot are the Work Palace and Bubbling Well vital points, respectively, which are easily stimulated. In religious ceremonies, vigorous clapping, singing, and dancing usually induce trance-like states in the participants.

These are said to be the two most important vital point sets in the body. So important were these that in biblical times, the effective method of execution of criminals by the Roman soldiers involved the crucifixion of the condemned person. This method involved the nailing of the prisoner to an erected wooden cross by driving two nails through the centers of the palms (Work Palace vital points) spread to the sides, and a third nail driven through the center of both feet (Bubbling Well vital point). Jesus Christ and two thieves are recorded to have met such a fate in the Christian Bible, death coming after the ninth hour.

Death from a penetrating injury through these vital points is difficult to understand from the perspective of modern medicine and pathology, as the only structures beneath the points are small bones, small muscles, and small blood vessels. The resulting trauma would not be expected to cause any major or persistent hemorrhaging. Blood infection resulting from bacteria gaining entry into the body through these wounds would usually be expected to take days rather than nine hours to kill the unfortunate person. The more plausible alternative explanation would be the stagnation of ki flow at those injured points with the eventual disruption of the energy flow in other pathways and meridians, leading to death.

The Work Palace and Bubbling Well points are a double set of some of the most important points on the ki channels. They are the major vital points where the ki energy is concentrated as it flows into or exits the body. Anatomically, the Work Palace vital point in each palm coincides with the confluence where the radial and ulnar arteries unite to form an arcade in either hand from which further arise the digital arteries to supply blood to the fingers.

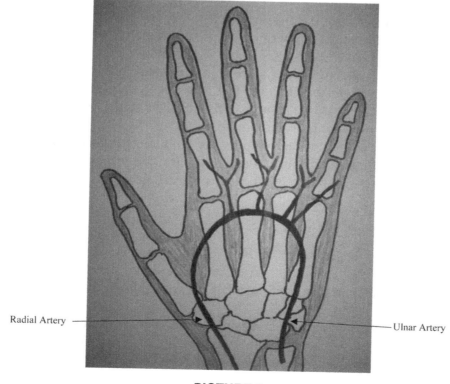

Radial Artery ———

——— Ulnar Artery

PICTURE 9
Arterial Blood Flow in the Hand

Similarly, each foot is supplied by the arcade of blood vessels formed from the confluence of the dorsalis pedis artery branch of the anterior tibial artery and the posterior tibial artery.

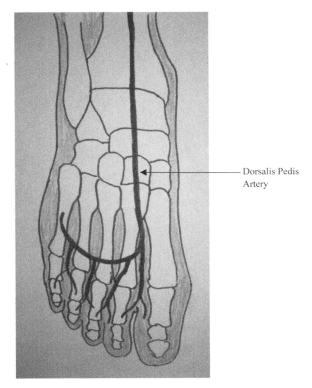

— Dorsalis Pedis Artery

PICTURE 10
Arterial Blood Flow in the Foot

It is well recognized that the walls of arteries possess the ability to generate electrical current when stretched by the turbulent blood flow at major arterial junctions. This is the piezo-electric effect, which is particularly strong at the bifurcation of the abdominal aorta in front of the fourth lumbar vertebrae as well as in the extensive arcade of blood vessels of the bowel arising from the superior mesenteric and inferior mesenteric arteries.

The combined length of small and large intestines is about twenty-eight feet, and this remarkable length of bowel is attached by thick connective tissue or mesentery in a broad, fan-like arrangement to a narrow fifteen centimeter root in the back of the abdomen. Even more interesting is the ability of the mesentery to rotate and fold the entire length of bowel into the small frame of the abdominal cavity. This structure has the most extensive arcade of blood vessels in the body, easily accommodating a quarter of the total blood volume of the body and arises from a root located in the center of the abdomen.

Other important blood vessel arcades include the Circle of Willis, which is the main supply of blood to the brain and coincides with the location of the Third Eye; the rich plexus of arteries of the Bend Center energy relay points are located in the back of the knees; the arch of the thoracic aorta in the chest gives off the major arterial branches through which flows at least fifty percent of the total blood volume to the head and upper limbs and which coincides with the location of the heart energy center; and the kidneys, with their unique blood flow through which a quarter of the body's blood volume flows. Piezo-electric activity at each of these sites makes it easy to recognize their potential for energy generation and transmission.

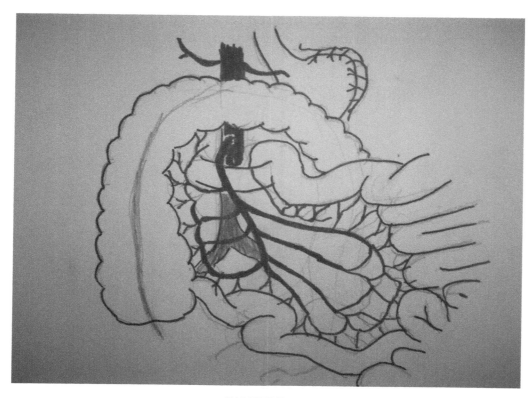

PICTURE 11
Arterial Blood Flow in the Abdominal Mesentery

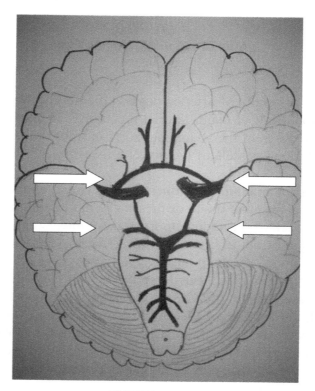

PICTURE 12
Arterial Flow of the Circle of Willis in the Brain

Other parts of the body, like bones, are capable of generating similar piezo-electric energy when subjected to stress, and this has been confirmed scientifically. Tendons are also piezo-electric because of their helical crystals. Taking advantage of this electrical property forms the basis of the Taoist practice of tendon lengthening and bone breathing exercises.

EMBRYOLOGICAL EVIDENCE

Life begins with the union of the sperm and the ovum and this is manifested as the prenatal ki energy, which is constant until death. In the early stages of life, the individual exists only as a collection of few dividing cells called the morula. More complex development occurs when the morula becomes a hollow ball or blastula with a pore at one end which soon develops into the anus, which in humans is the first organ to develop.

Subsequent development of the embryo creates the gastrula, which soon develops three distinct layers of cells from which all organs arise. These three germ layers are the endoderm or innermost layer, which gives rise to the digestive organs, lungs, and kidneys; the mesoderm or middle layer, which develops into the heart and circulatory system, muscles, and skeleton; and the outer layer or ectoderm, which develops into the brain and rest of the nervous system and skin. These layers are stacked one above the next, starting in the following order of the mesoderm, then the endoderm, and finally the ectoderm. With the close association of these layers, it is easy to postulate the existence of tiny pores that connect them to each other. Thus it is highly likely that at this prenatal stage of life there exist channels through which energy and information would flow and transfer between the dividing and maturing cells. It is also likely that the same microscopic channels would persist and function after birth as ki meridians.

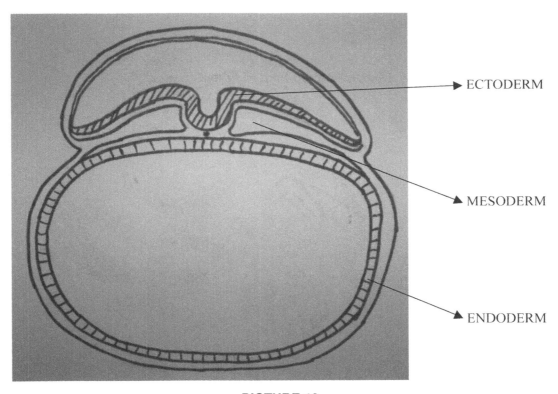

PICTURE 13
Human Embryo Picture Early Stage

A careful study of ki meridians indicate the flow of energy occurs between the skin and the internal organs with the exclusion of the brain. This observation is supported by the fact that the skin originates from the ectoderm, while the internal organs arise from the mesoderm and endoderm. It is important to note that though the skin and brain develop from the same ectodermal layer, both organs have no shared meridian link.

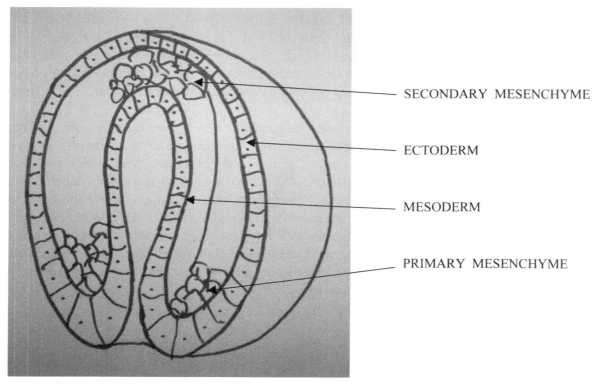

SECONDARY MESENCHYME

ECTODERM

MESODERM

PRIMARY MESENCHYME

PICTURE 14
Human Embryo Picture Early Stage

CHAPTER 8

BLACK BELT POOMSAE

The Taegeuk and Palgwe poomsae series have been designed to foster the following attributes in each practitioner prior to attaining the black belt and embarking on the journey of the study of advanced Taekwondo.

Character traits imbibed along the way include the laying of the spirit of solid foundation in the white belter as a template for the subsequent stages. After this is the "Lake" stage, which is manifested as inner firmness and outer softness. Next is the "Fire" stage, which encourages a sense of justice and ardor for training. The "Thunder," which is synonymous with great new-found power and dignity, is the fourth character trait developed after one or two years of training. This is accompanied by the "Wind" stage, where the student learns how to respond with strength or weakness as the occasion demands. The "Water" stage is the next important attribute and demonstrates how the student must show mental flexibility rather than stagnation to overcome all obstacles. Then the student should stand strong and firm as the "Mountain," enduring great physical and mental obstacles while his or her training is starting to root inside the heart.

The red belter is at an important crossroads, just reaching the end of the first part of the training and about to begin a second phase of learning. At this point he or she is expected to have perfected the basic Taekwondo skills with confidence while demonstrating maturity of character, humility, and honesty. Once the proper foundations are set and the above prerequisite ideals attained, the wiser and more mature student's training for the black belt stage can start in earnest.

The black belt is a phase that is greatly misunderstood by the lay public and even by the Taekwondo stylist. Rather than having achieved the pinnacle of one's training and abilities, it instead reinforces the reality that one's studies have only just started in earnest, like a transition from primary school to high school to university in pursuit of higher degrees.

Unlike the colored belt grades, where promotion examinations are conducted every few months, the dan grade student has to remain at each level for years before being considered eligible for a higher grade. This is to allow him or her to acquire more skilled knowledge and experience in their upward mobility, just as fine wine needs several years to mature into a delectable vintage. Compared to the keup grades patterns which have a strong emphasis on closed fist strikes, the yudanja and kodanja black belt poomsae have a surprisingly large number of open hand techniques. The clenched fists taught at junior levels condition the student to maintain a closed fist tension much of the time, concealing important pressure points in the palm and making it somewhat difficult for an adversary to trap the hand or apply a wrist lock. Many Taekwondo self-defense techniques usually begin with a wrist lock and then immobilization of the arm. On the other hand, the open palm allows the more mature student to strike faster and switch between techniques, such as joint locks and throws. It also allows precision finger tip strikes to small pressure point surface areas to disable the adversary.

The black belt poomsae have an increased number of sequences that teach ki energy techniques for healing and fighting needs. These are largely absent from the Palgwe poomsae and only introduced later in the more advanced Taegeuk Yuk Jang, Chil Jang, and Pal Jang. These constitute the Naegong or internal energy set of exercises and require intensive and dedicated practice as well as supervision from experienced masters to unlock the knowledge unique to each advanced poomsae.

For instance, the minimum period of learning before advancing from the first to the second dan black belt is one year. From the second to the third dan, the period lengthens to two additional years. The third dan black belt will need three years to advance to the fourth dan, then four more years to reach the fifth dan. The sixth dan black belt is achieved after five additional years, and then the seventh dan level requires a further seven years of training to be achieved. The seventh dan would require a minimum of seven years to reach the next level of the eighth dan. The last stage, or ninth dan, is only achieved after eight more years, and at this stage the Taekwondo practitioner may have spent about forty years of regular training and dedication to this martial art.

Thus the mastery needed to make the Taekwondo techniques second nature takes many years to achieve, during which time the student is expected to remain dedicated and focused in his or her training. The close study of the black belt poomsae should reward the diligent student with enough material to fill out the various time periods spent at each grade, decreasing the possibility of boredom and loss of motivation. The following poomsae are required to be mastered at each black belt level:

First degree black belt pattern: Poomsae Koryo San, Poomsae Koryo Dae
Second degree black belt pattern: Poomsae Keumgang
Third degree black belt pattern: Poomsae Taebaek
Fourth degree black belt pattern: Poomsae Pyongwon
Fifth degree black belt pattern: Poomsae Sipjin
Sixth degree black belt pattern: Poomsae Jitae
Seventh degree black belt pattern: Poomsae Cheonkwon
Eighth degree black belt pattern: Poomsae Hansoo
Ninth degree black belt pattern: Poomsae Ilyeo

CHAPTER 9

KORYO POOMSAE

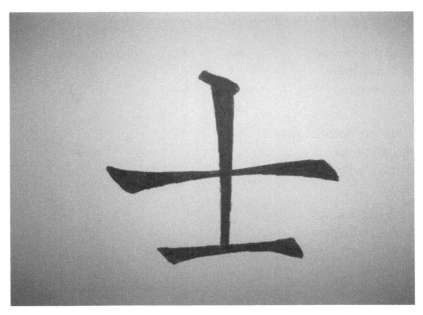

PICTURE 15
Koryo Poomsae Symbol

Koryo (A.D. 918-1392) was the ancient dynasty in korea,
And reknown for many things.
Koryo men first invented metal type,
and created the famous koryo ceramics.
Koryo men defeated the great Mongolians,
who ruled most of the ancient world.
Koryo men defended their land with great martial fortitude,
And at the same time were learned and righteous.
Koryo poomsae line means seonbae"a learned or man of virtue".

It is very important that in trying to understand the meaning of this poomsae, one must first understand the role of the "seonbae" in the context of Korean history.

The name seonbae means a virtuous scholar and the person was destined to become a high official of the state. Today's equivalent would be a senior and prestigious post in the Civil Service. The high regard attached to this position was such that several hundreds of scholars would study very hard for years to pass the difficult examinations, of which only a few were successful each time. The successful candidates would then become government officials and would live up to their reputation for integrity and incorruptibility. Unlike many of the ruling yangban class, who were often corrupt and greedy, the seonbae were mainly young men of integrity, possessing Confucian virtues of filial piety and loyalty to the king. They were devoid of private interest and despised wealth, and were always ready to lay down their lives to remain faithful to their principles and integrity.

The reference to the spirit of the Koryo Poomsae mentions the resistance of the Korean people and their great effort and sacrifice in repelling the invasion of the mighty Mongol army. This is epitomized in the poem "Songs of Flying Dragons," eulogizing the founders of the Choson Dynasty: General Yi Songgye (1335–1408), Mokcho (d. 1274), Ikcho, Tojo (1367–1422), Hwanjo (1315–1361), and Yi Pangwon (1367–1422): "Korea's six dragons flew in the sky/Their every deed was blessed by heaven/Their deeds tallied with those of sage kings."

Despite not being a scholar, General Yi Sonngye urged his son Yi Pangwon to study the classics; the latter passed the final civil service examination in 1383.

80. Though he was busy with war,
He loved the way of the scholar.
His work of achieving peace
Shone brilliantly.

81. He did not boast of his natural gifts,
His learning was equally deep.
The vast scope of royal works
Was indeed great.

82. Upon receiving an old scholar
He knelt down with due politeness.
What can you say about
His respect for scholarship?

Particular reference is made to Yi Songgye in subsequent verses, recalling his efforts in halting successive waves of foreign invaders: the Red Turbans in 1351, the Mongols in 1362 and 1370, and the Japanese pirates in 1377, 1380, and 1382.

88. He hit the backs of forty tailed deer.
He pierced the mouths and eyes of the rebels.
He shot down three mice from the eaves,
Were there any like him in the past?

This verse refers to Yi Songgye's shooting skills, where he shot forty deer on a hunting trip in Haeju in 1385 and his campaign against the Mongol minister Naghacu in 1362, where he shot the rebels in the mouth.

It is with great pride that the Korean people remember their effort to withstand the aggression of the Mongol army, the greatest and most modern fighting force the world had ever seen up to that point in time.

From 1200 A.D., the Golden Hordes, the name given to the great invading army from Mongolia, had ravaged and pillaged half of the uncivilized world, their dominance extending from Southeast Asia across the steppes of Russia, conquering China and linking Arabia via the silk trade routes, ending in the western boundary of Hungary. Along the way to full dominance, they had created the most modern military force, introducing for the first time the metric system into their formations, which were organized into an inverted pyramid structure of strength. From flexible units of ten soldiers, ascending to a platoon strength of 100, then a regimental strength of 1,000, a brigade strength of 5,000, a division strength of 10,000, organizing everything under an army corps of 100,000 soldiers.

Turning this army into an awesome crushing force, they utilized a very modern fighting strategy with the introduction of the fast, light cavalry, relying on expert nomad horsemen. Each warrior would possess up to five Mongolian horses and be able to advance at five times the pace of most opposing armies by riding all day at full speed, only stopping to exchange an exhausted horse for a rested one. They were lightly armed with bows, arrows, swords, and lances, able to fire their arrows with great accuracy without dismounting. The Mongol warriors frequently adopted a devastatingly deceptive strategy of tactical retreat, only to wheel their cavalry around to destroy their overconfident opponents.

The Mongols also excelled in psychological warfare, ruthlessly decimating their opponents, allowing only a few survivors to spread tales of terror to undermine the morale of the next besieged city. Europe was only saved from invasion by the River Danube, which lay in their path, and the cancellation of the Mongol campaign after the unexpected death of their undefeated military leader, Genghis Khan.

Their advance through Southeast Asia was also thwarted by the Koryo men, who were described as people of strong conviction and will. Koryo thus remained the only other territory that eluded capture by the Mongols. This action of the Koryo men is immortalized in the spirit of the seonbae as a strong martial spirit as well as a righteous man's spirit.

The first technique in Koryo Poomsae is the tong milgi jumbi seogi, which involves summoning great energy from the danjun to gouge an opponent's eyes and break free from his frontal bear hug. It also symbolizes the desperate will demonstrated by the people of Koryo in fighting off the destructive armies of the Mongols.

The action of the tong milgi also represents the energy path through the Thrusting Vessel, which is one of the eight extraordinary meridians of ki circulation around the body. The Thrusting Vessel is located in the core of the body, rising up like a hollow tube in front of the spinal cord from the perineum to the crown point, and encloses the seven major energy centers of the body. Energy may be raised along this channel in four stages.

The first stage starts from the perineum to the diaphragm and is used to transfer the original essence or pre-birth ki of the body through the lower danjun or lower energy center. The second one also starts from the perineum and ends at the neck, and involves the transfer of the postnatal ki energy generated from food and air through the middle danjun. The third draws from the perineum to the crown point and is used to raise the spirit energy to the upper danjun. The tong milgi involves the second stage where the ki is pushed upward along this tube and transferred to the solar plexus. This energy center is associated with power, spirit, freedom, and ego. From the solar plexus center it is further channeled to fortify the hands.

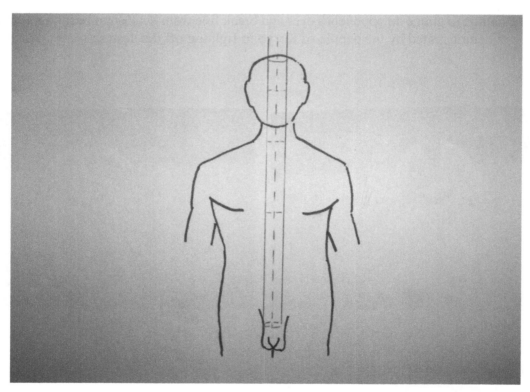

PICTURE 16
The Thrusting Vessel

The energy within the Thrusting Vessel can be moved further during a fourth stage, which involves raising it up to exit the crown point and gathering it in the Work Palace point of the right palm. This ki is brought down as the arms descend and transferred into the left hand in front of the perineum to be returned to the danjun.

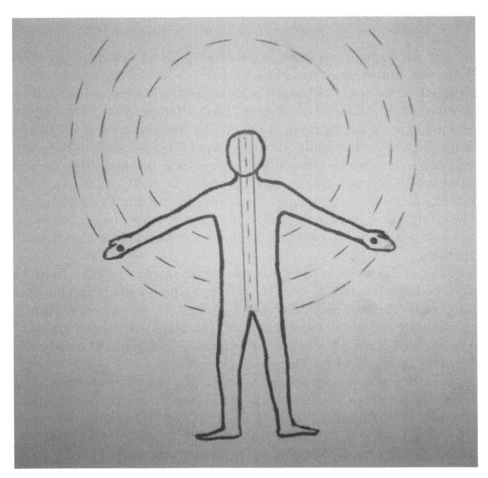

PICTURE 17
Ki Energy Flow Through Thrusting Vessel

POOM EXERCISE NO. 49

The year is 1362 and the Mongol marauders have invaded a sizable part of the Koryo Kingdom. The refugee is dressed in tattered clothes, once white flowing robes typical of the Korean elite, and has fled from the advancing pincer attack of the world's strongest army led by the Mongolian General Naghacu. His robes have become dusty brown from rolling in the dirt and bush after escaping from capture at the hands the small unit of eight of the foreign-speaking enemy soldiers. His weapons are lost and likewise his prize horse somewhere between the thick of the last battle and his present hiding place. He is relieved that he hasn't lost the sealed orders entrusted in his care by General Yi Songgye, who is marshalling the main defenses of the peninsula. The seonbae is Yi Songgye's distant cousin but he is treated like a trusted son, having grown up within his household. The scroll feels safe against the warmth of his skin as he trudges through the craggy mountainous countryside. For now, he is in the safety of a band of other hungry young men who had found themselves separated and lost from their fighting units as the Mongol invaders run rampant over large swathes of Koryo territory.

It is already nightfall but the moon is hidden by the dense smoke that rises from the sacked and still burning Koryo village. The darkness is lit by the sparks from burning timber crackling in the distance as his group approaches cautiously. The redness of the night's embers and the nauseating smell of burning flesh draw him like a beacon to the site of the latest massacre. The victims are those who couldn't run away as soon as the enemy entered the village. They are innocent children, women, and elderly men cut down by the ruthless sabers, lying in mangled and twisted shapes in the village.

The sight of the dead raises a wave of anger and hatred at the wanton destruction wrought by Naghacu's forces. He feels the resolve set in his face as the energy rises from the depths of his bowels, flooding in waves to warm his palms. He realizes that the Mongol enemy may be back to continue their looting of the sacked village. After saying final prayers for the dead, he and the other lost warriors turn away from the scene of destruction and melt into the darkness of the night once again.

Three days and three nights pass as he witnesses countless sights of terrible destruction on Koryo soil. Hundreds of villages in the path of the advancing Mongolian army are put to the sword. The fate of the few survivors is obvious. They will suffer hideous torture at the hands of their captors. It would have been better if they were already dead.

On the fourth day, his group is ambushed by a small enemy force that springs down from hiding above the walls of a narrow canyon cut by nature through the mountain range of the northern Koryo territory. The enemy's blood-curdling cries buffet him and his companions, followed by a hail of arrows which scatter their party. As he picks himself from the moss-covered soil, a Mongolian warrior rushes at him, aiming his bloodied lance at the seonbae's stomach. His foreign eyes blaze with bloodlust and cruelty as he attempts to impale him.

The Koryo man's surprise and fear evaporate from his mind as the years of tough training at the hands of his master kick in. He shifts sideways, evading the weapon's thrust. The determined Mongol soldier recovers from his miss and kicks at him. Again the young Koryo man steps forward fearlessly and strikes downward at the Yin vital point of the spleen meridian (Sea of Blood) above his knee with his left knife-hand, parrying his kick harmlessly to the side. Then he thrusts his right hand into the Yin vital point on the enemy's Adam's apple with all his strength, crushing his wind-pipe. He follows quickly with a powerful kick to the intersection of the Yin meridians of the spleen and kidney in the enemy warrior's groin to dissipate his ki energy. As the Mongol drops to the ground, the seonbae paralyzes him with a downward left palm thrust to his knee joint, breaking it, and then he destroys his ankle by wrenching his foot. He finishes him off by turning around and stomping his left heel down into the enemy's chest, crushing his sternum.

Yi Songgye's teaching about using Yin and Yang vital point principles in attacking sequentially below and above the waist flashes through his mind as he stares at the crumpled shape of his enemy.

POOM EXERCISE NO. 50

After knocking a second Mongol warrior down on his knees, the seonbae steps behind the enemy, summoning that vital energy again into his hands. His open hands feel as hard as the strongest Koryo steel. He cups the enemy's head in one hand and swings his clenched fist down to smash into his temple, breaking his skull. Momentarily, an image flashes through his fevered mind…the Koryo fist crushing the spirit of the Mongol invasion.

The upward-sweeping arm movements indicate the flow of the ki energy from the perineum through the Thrusting Vessel to the upper danjun in the brain. The practitioner is able to suck the ki energy from the perineum and up the spine in stages to nourish the upper danjun in the brain. During this fourth stage of circulating the energy within the Thrusting Vessel, the ki is raised up to exit the crown point and gathered in the Work Palace point of the right palm. This powerful ki is transferred into the left fist and brought down as the arms descend to the front of the perineum to be returned to the danjun.

POOM EXERCISE NO. 51

There is no time to savor his small victory as a third Mongol rushes at him from behind with his battle axe raised. The now-exhausted seonbae spins around to engage him and ducks to avoid the enemy's charge, forcing the axe swing to miss its mark. Wielding his left arm like his lost sword, the young Koryo man slashes at the Mongol's face in great fury, blinding him. Then he strikes down at the warrior's lower body with the same knife-hand, sending him stumbling backward, off balance.

He jumps on him, slashing furiously with his right knife-hand, cutting through the enemy's defenses at different angles, first into the Yin vital point of the liver meridian in the side of his neck and down at the Yin vital point of the spleen meridian (Winnower Gate) in his mid-thigh. He pursues him backward with indignant rage, using the punishing onslaught of his powerful knife-hand. He strikes back with the spirit of righteousness and conviction. Every blow is thrown with full force to recover his occupied lands.

Slash…strike…crush…

Slash…strike…crush…until every last Mongol warrior is driven off.

Finish him off by crushing his throat with the tiger-mouth strike.

His mind strays again to his master… The attack utilizes Yang and Yin to strike above and below the waist, as well as on the left and right sides.

POOM EXERCISE NO. 52

The battle seems to last forever as confusion reigns in the tight mountain pass. Another enemy soldier forces him back with wild thrusting attacks with his lance. He easily evades the snarling Mongol by shifting back out of range of the sharp metal tip and simultaneously deflecting each lance thrust by chopping and knocking the weapon to the side. He retreats continuously under the force of the attack, chopping and striking vital points to weaken the enemy's arms before turning the tables around on him. He spins around as the Mongol soldier makes a final thrust, catching him off balance, and smashes the intersection point of the Yang meridians of the large intestine and gall bladder located in his temple with his back-fist, crushing his skull. Then he slashes at enemy's neck with his knife-hand, forcing him backward with his counter-offensive.

He attacks Yin and Yang vital points in sequence from the arms rising up to the head and neck. His strikes follow the cycle of destruction with the activation of pericardium, triple heater (fire), large intestine (metal), liver (wood), spleen (earth), and kidney (water) points in that sequence.

Strike high, slash low,
Until the enemy is pushed back.
Strike high, slash low,
Until the Hordes are out of the peninsula.
Strike high, slash low,
Strike hard with righteous determination.
Slash…strike…crush…

Slash…strike…crush…every step of the way. Through every Koryo village and across every river. Pushing them off every inch of Koryo soil. Until every last Mongol warrior is driven out.

Finish him off with two powerful kicks and punches to his vital points.

All around him are sights of the dead and dying enemy soldiers lying broken in the mountain pass. Also lying amongst them are the easily recognizable bodies of some of the young Koryo men who have been his companions in the last few days. Their white robes are stained crimson as they lie in the pools of their ultimate sacrifice. A great exhilaration rises amongst the other surviving Koryo warriors as they realize that the Mongol enemy has retreated in confusion. They rush after them in full pursuit, determined to chase the world's strongest army out of Koryo. The seonbae collapses to the ground in sheer exhaustion, falling on the body of one of the enemy.

NOTES

_____

_____

_____

_____

_____

_____

_____

_____

CHAPTER 10

KEUMGANG POOMSAE

PICTURE 18
Keumgang Poomsae Symbol

Keumgang-san the most beautiful mountain in the Korean peninsula,
Rising from the sea and ending in the rock of ten thousand forms
Keumgang has the hardness of diamonds
And its inner beauty visible from every angle.
It gives its name to the Keumgang Yoksa or mightiest warrior,
As named by the Buddha.
Keumgang poomsae is solid and powerful,
befitting a second dan black belter's dignity.

The year is 1968 and the young jeweler's assistant is just completing the day's task of polishing the store's gem stones in Seoul, the capital city of South Korea. A postcard has just arrived from his cousin Choi, who emigrated to America a few years earlier. The beautiful-looking card was delivered just in time for the Korean national holiday of Gwangbokjeol, or Liberation Day. He becomes very excited after reading the words scribbled in the common Korean Hangul alphabet, and is pleased to realize that his cousin is alive and doing well somewhere in Detroit in the industrial heartland of America. He has just opened his second Taekwondo gym in that city full of Americans hungry to learn this dynamic martial art from

Korea. They had both trained in one of the Chung Do Kwan gyms in Seoul achieving the grade of fourth dan black belt.

He pockets the postcard then retrieves it again from his shirt, peering closely at its front picture in the subdued lighting of the inner office. Another realization hits him suddenly. It bears the sharp image of a majestic looking mountain, so real and alive that it looks like its sharp jagged slopes are slicing through the postcard paper. Its snow-covered peak is pearl white, glinting from the early morning sunrays. It jolts an indelible memory in his mind, appearing familiar to him as it always did to every person born of Korean blood.

This is definitely the Keumgang-san, the most beautiful mountain in all of Korea and also regarded by all as the center of the national spirit. It is located in the middle of the Taebaek mountain range in what is now known as North Korea. The last time he saw it was many years ago, just before the Korean peninsula split in two and he was forced with his parents to flee to the south to begin a new life.

His mind is transported back to the happy days of his childhood when his cousin Choi and he would race each other up the rocky sides of the mountain that dominated their simple rustic village. In those days, Korea was still under Japanese domination and everything Korean was suppressed. Not that it mattered much to him as an eight-year-old. He was only interested in things that were important to an eight-year-old, like learning to whistle like the birds, disobeying his mother by climbing the trees, or clambering up into the mountains tightly wrapped in warm clothing to ward off the cold breeze that flowed down its sides.

How thoughtful of cousin Choi, he thinks. Other memories of their childhood enter his mind, like when they both wandered too far up into the mountains, getting lost in its eerie charms while trekking for hours from one beguiling peak to another. An elderly wood cutter had brought an end to their escapade, taking them both home to worried parents and sharp tongues.

PICTURE 19
Outer Keumgang Mountain with Manmulsan (Rock of Ten Thousand Forms)

He again returns the postcard to his pocket and turns his attention to the diamond ring in his hand, twisting it slowly through 360 degrees, admiring every angle and cut. From multiple angles, the gemstone reflects back the soft jeweler's light, bringing forth a different brilliant reflection from its depth; an opal blue glint changes to red sapphire, then to white platinum, each fire as different from the next.

Keumgang-san looks magnificent from all angles, 1,638 meters high in Kangwon-do, North Korea. It covers 400 square kilometers, running sixty kilometers in length with a width of forty kilometers from east to west. It consists of granite and diorite, weathered over centuries into a variety of shapes such as the 12,000 picturesque stone formations, ravines, cliffs, stone pillars, and peaks. It has always been rooted to this site, from the beginning of creation, enduring the millennia and as permanent as a diamond stone.

Inner Keumgang is compared to a woman's beauty, noted for its sweet enchanting and breathtaking views like Manpok Ravine, and Outer Keumgang is likened to masculine beauty, featuring large peaks including Chipson Peak of Manmulsang (Rock of Ten Thousand Forms), which is well known for its many waterfalls. Then there is the exciting Sea Keumgang enveloping pristine serene lagoons and stone pillars.

PICTURE 20
Serene Beauty of Sea Keumgang

There is an old Korean adage that says "One cannot die before he sees Mount Keumgang." Keumgang-san undergoes a magnificent transformation according to the season. In spring, it is named Keumgang, and various flowers are in bloom, sparkling like diamonds, hence its name. In summer, it is called Pongraesan, meaning the place where a spirit lives. Then, its sheer cliffs are enveloped by drifting clouds, wrapped in green foliage and full of singing birds. During autumn, it is called Phungaksan (great mountain of coloured leaves), and in winter, Kaegolsan (stone bone mountain).

Several ancient legends have grown up as permanent as the Keumgang-san. There is the legend of the Keumgang Yeoksa (the Keumgang Warrior) as named by the Buddha, who represents the mightiest warrior. At the entrance to the Sokguram Grotto in the Bulguksa Temple in Kyongju, there are stone carvings of two warriors representing the Keumgang Yeoksa performing Keumgang makki.

PICTURE 21
Keumgang Yeoksa (Keumgang Warrior) at the Bulguksa Templa

LEGEND OF KURYONG POND

The Kuryong (nine dragons) Falls is a sheer drop of seventy-four feet with a width of four meters. It is one of the largest waterfalls in Keumgang Mountain and a pond below the falls is known as the Kuryong Pond. Legend has it that one of nine dragons went there to defend the Keumgang Mountain.

POOM EXERCISE NO. 53

The attack comes as soon as he closes the jewelry shop for the day, locking its shutters. Five odd-looking men stand together, then two break away and cross the deserted street behind him as he struggles to lock the stiff bolt of the entrance door. Funny how he hadn't noticed them moments earlier, he wonders before they close in on him. As they surround the jeweler's assistant, it dawns on him that it's a robbery; the store has a fortune in gems, millions of won worth and a prime target for greedy fingers.

The first hoodlum grabs his hands from the front in a vice grip. The shop assistant's resolve hardens and his eyes become unfathomable as he drops his hands and launches a pre-emptive bak chigi or head butt strike at the assailant's face. Before the attacker can recover, he twists his wrists out of the robber's grip and smashes his palm-heel into his jaw. He continues with rapid counter-attacks, knocking him out with multiple open palm midline strikes to the chest and solar plexus.

POOM EXERCISE NO. 54

Then he defeats the second robber's attempt to grapple by stepping backward to evade his arms. He chops the Yin vital point of the thief's right lower bicep, paralyzing his arm. Then he pulls him off balance by stepping backward and strikes the identical spot on his other arm. After weakening his arms, he hits the Protuberance Assistance vital point of the liver meridian on the side of the opponent's neck with his powerful knife-hand strike.

With the robber dazed, he spins him around by turning his shoulders to trap his hands behind his back. This sudden maneuver positions him behind the second attacker and changes the direction of his counterattacks by exposing a new set of vital points on his back. It also resembles the pose of the mighty Keumgang Warrior as he thrusts his knee forcefully upward into the second man's kidney to incapacitate him. The attacks follow Yang and Yin principle, alternating between right and left, front and back.

The Keumgang makki or diamond block technique demonstrates the black belter's ability to develop stable balance and a solid rooted stance. It involves using the mind and special breathing methods to transfer the ki from the danjun down into the ground to anchor the martial artist firmly to the earth.

Then he seizes his attacker in a side head lock and rolls over his back to finish him off with a neck break. This maneuver emphasizes the powerful rooting of the horseback stance. The martial artist can visualize deep roots extending from the Bubbling Well points in the soles of both feet, growing deep into the ground like a giant tree which has anchored itself firmly to the earth, withstanding powerful winds and earthquakes over many centuries. The mind leads the ki down into the ground at three points, including a vertical link through the perineum in the center into the earth, as well as down the legs on both sides. Even when the legs are uprooted as the martial artist spins, the black belter remains rooted through the middle ki link between the perineum and earth.

POOM EXERCISE NO. 55

He is grabbed from behind in a rear full nelson head lock by the third man who has joined the attack. The shop assistant pulls his attacker off balance by twisting sharply to the left and swings his right leg up in the air before stamping his foot down in the ground. He uses the upward reflected reaction force generated by his foot stamp coupled with the sinking of his center of gravity and simultaneous downward double elbow smash on his opponent's lower biceps to paralyze his arms and break free, followed by a backward head butt into the third robber's face.

Before the hoodlum can recover, he turns to face him and grabs his collar in both hands using a crossed grip. Then he drops his weight into a horseback stance, pulling down the opponent and spinning him around with a twist of both arms to expose his back. The would-be victim sweeps his attacker off balance with his left foot and finishes him off by smashing his left hammer-fist into the robber's right temple (intersection point of large intestine and gall bladder meridians).

The attack uses the cycle of destruction: pericardium (fire) followed by large intestine (metal).

At the sight of their fallen accomplices and the uncompromising toughness of the would-be-victim's determination and fighting spirit, the remaining thugs lose their composure and beat a hasty retreat.

One important underlying theme of this poomsae is the exhibition of boldness and power on the part of the second degree black belt. It also demonstrates the inherent advantages of spinning the opponent through 180 degrees about their vertical axis, seeking to expose vital points for attack either from the front or back .This is similar to the analogy of being able to admire the multiple light reflections seen in a perfectly polished diamond, appreciable only from different angles.

3. Mountains are steadfast,
But waters are not so.
Since they flow day and night,
Can there be old waters?
Great heroes are like waters,
Once gone, they never return.
4. Blue mountains speak of my desire,
Green waters reflect my lover's love:
Green waters may flow away,
But can blue mountains change?
Green waters too cannot forget blue mountains,
They wander through in tears.

—Hwang Chini (c. 1506–1544)

NOTES

_____

_____

_____

_____

_____

_____

CHAPTER 11

TAEBAEK POOMSAE

PICTURE 22
Taebaek Poomsae Symbol

Tangun founded the nation of Korean people in Taebaek (Mount Baekdoo),
That was four thousand three hundred years ago.
The messenger symbolized the bridge between Heaven and the earth,
Spreading his lofty thought of "hongik ingan"(humanitarian ideal).
Taebaek poomsae was created in his honor,
Meaning the sacred light from Heaven that illuminates the earthly darkness.
Each movement should be nimble and precise,
Yet performed with rigor and determination.

There are different myths concerning the origin of the Korean people, each one as varied as the next, but a few threads of commonality run through these stories.

In one of the popular versions, there was a god named Hwanin living in the heavens. He had a son, Hwanung, who peered over the edge of heaven down into earth each day to observe men. Each time, he would shed tears as he worried for the fate of mortals, wishing to rule them in order to bring peace and justice to mankind. His father Hwanin was moved and allowed him to descend into the world, carrying three seals or heavenly heirlooms, three sacred bronze items including a mirror, a dagger, and a bell, as well as 3,000 servants. In addition, he ordered the three lords of wind, rain, and clouds to follow him and instructed them to teach the people more than 360 useful arts, including agriculture, medicine, moral principles, and a code of law.

Hwanung descended into the world, arriving on the top of Mount Taebaek, establishing a city called Shinshi, meaning "City of the Gods." There, two beasts approached him, wishing to be human, and these were the tiger and the bear. He instructed them to remain in a dark cave for a hundred days without seeing the daylight and gave both a handful of mug wort and twenty pieces of garlic with which to stave off hunger. The tiger was temperamental and ran away before the end of the ordeal, while the bear was patient to the end, eventually turning into a beautiful woman named Ungnyeo.

After her transformation, she craved a child but no one was willing to wed her, as she was once a beast. She sat beneath a sandalwood tree in sadness praying every day for a child. Hwanung was moved by her prayers, taking human form to give her a son named Dangun, who became the founder of the Korean people.

Dangun, being the bridge between heaven and earth, established his kingdom called Asadal, meaning "the place where the morning shines." The name was later changed to Joseon, and he is said to have lived for 1,908 years, ruling for 1,500 years before retiring to the quiet of the mountains to become a divine spirit of the mountain or Sansillyeong.

From factual documentation and historical evidence, modern Koreans are probably the descendants of migrating tribes originating in Manchuria or Siberia in Central Asia. After moving southward, they settled along the great rivers and on the east and south coasts of the Korean peninsula. Heaven in their myths may be referring to the initial lands where their ancestors originated, and earth is the mountainous Korean peninsula where they finally settled.

Further evidence suggests that the Go Joseon kingdom founded in 2333 B.C. was comprised of three tribes including the Hwanung tribe, the Bear tribe, and the Tiger tribe. Northeastern Korea extending to eastern Manchuria was the traditional dwelling place for those who believed in the Tiger totem, and the Manchu-Tungusic people in Siberia had the Bear totem.

To this day in Korea, the third of October is celebrated as Gaecheon-jeol, a day marked to pay tribute to Dangun, who founded Joseon. To some Koreans, Dangun would be considered the equivalent of the American president, Queen Elizabeth, the Pope, and the Japanese emperor all rolled into one.

Ancient Korean religion predates Buddhism and centers on the role of the shaman or medicine man. The shaman was usually the warrior king who could intercede with the heavenly or spiritual forces on behalf of the tribe. The spirit of a god or dead ancestor could be invoked to possess the shaman in special trance-like rituals and dances often held on mountain tops with the aim of bringing good fortune and to ward off ill through manipulation of these spirits. The shaman was considered the bridge between heaven and the earth, able to connect like a messenger from the human world to the world of spirits.

According to the Korean origin myth, the three sacred bronze objects are the same that feature as part of the magical tools of the shaman. These are the mandolin dagger, a symbol of secular authority which was used to banish evil; the knobbed mirror, used to move the gods of the sun; and the bell or rattle, used to bring together heaven and earth. Much later the role of the king and shaman were separated and no longer held by the same individual.

Aside from the above history of the Korean race and its contribution to the philosophy behind Taebaek poomsae, the crane plays an even more important role. White cranes in Korean folklore are known as companions of the Daoist immortals, acting as messengers that can communicate between the worlds…the bridge between the Heaven and the earth.

These key references reveal a deep philosophy based on ancient Taoist beliefs. The universe is thought to be composed of stars, galaxies, and other heavenly bodies which are held in a cosmos bound and surrounded

PICTURE 22A
White Cranes

by ki energy. This includes our own planet Earth, which is similarly invested by this heavenly energy. Every creature and inanimate object is thought to be surrounded and permeated by this universal energy, maintaining a link to the greater cosmic force. Asian philosophy teaches that this heavenly energy can be drawn into the body, passing through the crown of the head by opening up the crown point and extending one's own ki field upward to merge with the universal external ki. The practitioner is required to inhale, simultaneously using the mind to draw in the external ki energy, stopping at the crown point before exhaling.

The next inhalation draws this heavenly energy inside, flowing downward in the midline over the back of the head to rest just below the spine of the seventh cervical vertebrae (the Great Hammer point), which is the junction between the neck and the shoulders. During the following exhalation, the universal energy is retained there and not allowed to disperse.

The second half of this exercise involves inhaling and dropping one's ki energy down to the legs and through the two Bubbling Well points in the center of the soles of both feet, into the ground to link up with the greater earth energy. The next breath is then used to draw up the earth energy through the legs to the Great Hammer point. With each breathing cycle the energy is slowly accumulated there until it feels full. Then the combined heavenly and earthly ki energies are directed out to the Work Palace point in the center of the palms while extending the arms outward to the sides during exhalation before being transferred to the danjun through the hands.

This poomsae is a compilation of self-defense techniques that closely mirror the unique fighting techniques of the Flying Crane version of the Fukien White Crane. It requires precision in its hunting skills, which are described by some as one strike/one kill. Its nimble steps allow it to evade larger, more powerful predators; a determined will makes it stand motionless on one foot in water for any length of time to deceive any passing fish, which would usually be speared in an instantaneous single strike.

The crane style fighting techniques are derived from eight principles which include swallowing, spitting, floating, sinking, pouncing, lifting, throwing, and springing.

Swallowing techniques involve the ability to absorb and redirect an incoming force using, for example, four ounces to topple 1,000 pounds. Spitting refers to the defender's reaction, like counter-attacking with a finger tip strike after disturbing the attacker's rhythm and balance. Floating means the upward motion of the limbs while maintaining connection to the earth and is used to lift and control an opponent's blow. The ki can be sunk into the danjun using breathing methods, and this along with the sinking of the body, hands, and feet in combination with a spitting attack is a characteristic movement in this fighting method.

Pouncing involves rushing the hands out to intercept, grasp, and strike, while lifting means raising the hands to intercept or strike. Throwing is used as a technique to knock and clear the opponent's limb out of the way utilizing a powerful action from the defender's arm, while springing energy is used to block or strike. These methods are always accompanied by the precise and nimble steps suitable for evasion and split second counters.

The first technique in the poomsae is the sonnal area hecho makki and illustrates the above principles. It uses arm wing-like movement and a stepping technique to incorporate the four principles of swallowing (inhaling), spitting (exhaling), lifting, and sinking. These circular motions are used to break an opponent's balance and redirect his force.

POOM EXERCISE NO. 56

Imagine the attacker has grabbed your shirt front with both hands. Bring your palms together above his and turn to the left in a cat stance to unbalance him. Force your arms down to both sides, knocking his arms apart to break his grip. Counter-attack his exposed center line with a groin kick and double blows to the body.

The stepping technique is unique to the white crane method and is performed with the cat stance. This stance involves placing the ball of the lead foot in light contact with the floor with the knee of the supporting leg bent and the pelvis tucked in. It is a highly mobile stance, allowing the defender to quickly transition to positions in any direction and can be used to sink the body and add force to a crank motion or joint lock of the opponent's seized limb. Stepping from this posture involves initially dropping the heel to contact the floor rather than sliding the foot forward, and this helps explosive energy transfer into the punch or kick that follows.

It is believed that this posture helps to align the spinal cord and activate the energy centers of the body. Ki is said to flow more easily first from the head, spine, and ribs and then to the arms, legs, pelvis, and shoulders. It involves the activation of the liver meridian, which stretches from the big toe carrying Yin energy through the inside of the leg and thigh, then passing close to the danjun to end at the lungs.

POOM EXERCISE NO. 57

Step 5 reveals a similar set of techniques found in this fighting style. Jebipoom Mok Chigi (swallow form knife-hand strike) utilizes the principle of swallowing while simultaneously lifting and spitting to deflect and counter-attack fiercely against an opponent's strike.

In Step 6, the technique of sonnal opeo japki (grabbing) is also an example of throwing, which knocks the opponent's limb out of the way to expose the vital points on his body. These weak points are immediately exploited through springing action to unleash a focused powerful strike. Block his punch upward with your left palm, hitting the inside of his wrist where the three Yin vital points of the lung, heart, and pericardium meridians are found and strike the fourth Yin vital point (liver 18) in the side of his neck with your right knife-hand. Then, thrust his left arm away to expose his center line and attack the fifth Yin vital point in his solar plexus. This attack activates the cycle of destruction from pericardium and heart (fire), lung (metal), liver (wood), and spleen (earth).

In ki energy training, the hand technique involves shaking and quivering the fingers to draw a large flow of the bio-electric energy to the hands, just as the white crane would shake the water drops vigorously from its feathers after diving in water for prey. Similarly, the shaman dances and spins, running with light foot-steps while rattling small bells in his hands to invoke and mediate with the spirits bears a close resemblance to the shivering crane bird.

POOM EXERCISE NO. 58

Steps 9 through 13 indicate the defender's reaction to an attacker's surprise double wrist grab from behind. Raise both hands and slip behind him in a similar posture to Keumgang montong makki. Then twist and force your right hand behind his shoulder to free your wrist dangkyo teok jireugi (uppercut punch). Punch his side to break his ribs , then pull him forward with dol-tzeogi (hinge technique) and strike his head. Knock him down with a kick to the back of his knees followed by an elbow strike to the head before applying a rear naked choke.

Taebaek poomsae may be performed with light and nimble steps, as if one has taken the form of the white crane. It may mimic the dance of Dangun, the shaman king and founder of the Korean people, and the set of movements in Steps 9 through 13 bear resemblance to the ritual trance-like steps a Korean shaman performed when exorcising bad spirits from a tormented individual.

The medicine man is on the summit of Mount Paektu, clad in thick robes sewn from animal fur, and he stalks over the cold, rocky ground with the nimble sure steps of the white crane bird. The early morning mist has just drifted away, allowing the first light of the morning sun to bathe the mountain top. Every few seconds he pauses suddenly before darting off in a new direction with a spin and finally approaches the middle-aged female member of his tribe who is kneeling on the frost-covered ground. She has been suffering from regular nose bleeds and severe headaches, forcing her to go berserk and attack her children sometimes. In his hands are small bronze bells clutched firmly, making a rattling noise that would either call the heaven spirits to earth or banish the malevolent spirits from his domain. He is careful to avoid letting the bells fall out of his hands by twisting his wrists smoothly from side to side as he spins and dances to the beat of the small drum held by his assistant. He sings his songs and continues his self-purification exercise of washing off bad spirits from his body, starting from the upper body and ending at his feet.

As he sings, he calls the name of the bad spirit which has been dwelling within the poor suffering woman. He describes it as taking the form of a grasshopper with the hair of a woman and tiger's teeth. It has an impenetrable breast plate of bronze and its tail has stingers like a scorpion's, which it uses to torment the woman. This malevolent spirit rises within its victim, beating its wings like the sound of horses running to battle. He can see its form inside the victim's wild eyes.

The medicine man stops abruptly in his steps and retrieves his other tools from his assistant—a bronze shaman's mirror with a perfectly polished surface and a knob handle on its opposite side, and a sacred mandolin dagger. He promptly hides them within his robes and begins to dance more slowly with the same precise body motions. He drops his hands, spreading them apart in a circular motion that appears as if he is freeing his wrists from the clutches of the spirit he is battling.

He turns his body away from the anguished woman, concealing his hands at his waist, and pulls out the sacred dagger and knobbed mirror out of her sight. His face is grim as he readies to finally face the powerful spirit.

PICTURE 23
Korean Shaman Exorcising a Bad Spirit

He whirls around in a sudden sharp turn and with his well-practiced hands he aims the reflection of the sun's rays expertly off the well-polished mirror surface into the eyes of the bad spirit to ward it off. His intention is to use the mirror to move the gods of the sun into the face of the malevolent spirit, dazzling it, and with the dagger in his other hand, banish the evil one. He lifts the weapon high and draws in the evil spirit. With his lead arm he uses the cutting thrust of the dagger to destroy it. Then he spins away from the woman and makes a loud cry of triumph, staggering away from the scene of his mock battle.

POOM EXERCISE NO. 59

Steps 19 through 21 consist of the techniques of sonnal montong makki (double knife-hand block), nullo makki (pressing block), pyonsonkkeut sewotzireugi (vertical finger tip strike), japhin son mok ppaegi (pulling out the caught wrist), and deung jumeok olgul bakkat chigi (outward back fist strike).

In the same sequence, these techniques illustrate the combined tactics of swallowing the opponent's attack, followed by pouncing and spitting by rushing out the hands to block and counter-attack with a finger tip strike to a vital point.

The opponent manages to trap your hand in his hands. Free your wrist by winding your body through a 180-degree counter-clockwise turn. Like a coiled-up spring, unleash a sudden powerful back fist strike to his temple (intersection of Yang meridians—large intestine and gall bladder meridians). Finish him off with a blow on the Yin vital point in his solar plexus. The attack sequence involves activation of Yang and Yin points.

NARYE KA (SONG OF EXORCISM)

On the day of the exorcism in Lord Nayong's hall,
The clowns dress in striped cloth of gold.
When there's a performance of the mountain kut,
Even the demons are arrayed in striped cloth of gold.
Ri-ra-ri-ro na-ri-ra ri-ra-ri.

NOTES

_____

_____

_____

_____

_____

_____

_____

_____

_____

_____

_____

CHAPTER 12

PYONGWON POOMSAE

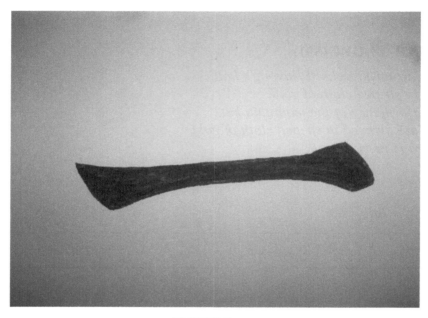

PICTURE 24
Pyongwon Poomsae Symbol

Pyongwon poomsae symbolizes the origin of life ,
And the transformation of the plain.
Fertile fields stretch over a vast area,
The source of life and fertility for all creatures.
Pyongwon poomsae begins with the overlapping hands,
Concentrating the force or vital essence in the source of human life.

The original name of this poomsae is said to have been Paekje hyung, named after Paekje, one of the three ancient unified kingdoms on the Korean peninsula. Paekje was known for its vast fertile plains and farmlands and five major grains were cultivated here including barley, rice, soybeans, foxtail millet, and millet. Of the lot, rice was king. Rice had historically been grown in the Korean peninsula and there is strong archeological data that indicates that the crop existed there as far back as 15,000 years ago, making it even earlier than the previous evidence that placed its first cultivation in China. It rapidly became the mainstay of the agriculture in part due to the ability of the rice grains to be preserved for a long time.

Just as in the wider Asian subcontinent and beyond, the rice crop was very important to the lives and structures of ancient Korean society. It was so important that even court officials, noblemen, and soldiers were usually paid their wages in rice. Honoring their ancestors and deities in ceremonies were usually accompanied by libations of rice. It was a common aphorism that health flowed from the rice plant. With a bumper harvest, the people could be expected to remain healthy, including the young couples whose fertility was dependent on their nutritional health. This link between the rice crop and fertility was recognized from ancient times within Asia, and even in the rice fields, the Chinese peasants were sometimes known to copulate in order to improve their harvest. Just as human life sprang from within the loins, so did the agricultural yield spring from the earth. In a bad harvest year, people would starve or die in great numbers and birth rates would plummet.

A recurring theme evident in the study of Pyonwon poomsae is its resemblance to the ritualistic dance performed at harvest time by the village shaman in honor of the earth deity's gift of a bountiful rice harvest. In later centuries this was transformed into the farmers' music or nongak, which is a very energetic dance with motions that mimic the different uses of farming and harvesting implements, and involves traipsing with fleet steps and acrobatic spins under the goading beat of drums.

The nongak dance was usually performed in twelve parts, including a small drum dance by young men, a human pyramid by children, a traditional flat drum dance by a group of people, an hourglass drum dance by both male and female dancers, a farm dance originating from ancient sorcerers danced by multiple people holding big floral fans, a most impressive sangmo dance by male dancers, and an imitative crane dance.

The white crane birds had a special significance to the ancient Korean tribes and were considered companions of the Daoist immortals, serving as messengers able to communicate to and from heaven. The white crane was revered for its ability to guard its vital essence. Just like humans, a male and female would pair and bond for life. This would be preceded by an elaborate courtship dance that involves agile displays, leaping in the air, spinning steps, and lots of whooping sounds: a fertility dance of the birds.

The typical instrument was the janggo or hourglass-looking drum, which is constructed with a body of an hourglass shape with double-ended drum skin heads, the male head on the right called the chae side covered with lighter horse hide to produce higher tones. The female head was on the opposite end and covered with thick cow hide to produce deep, low tones. The combination of a drum beat from both ends bears an allusion to human sexuality, which requires the merging of male and female for procreation. The proper rhythm of playing both ends of the drum invokes the male and female spirit in unison in the fertility dance.

The jumbi-seogi is the moa seogi wen kyop-son (or left overlapping hands), which concentrates ki energy in the sacral plexus or root chakra and lower abdomen in preparation for its release into the hands in the form of the tong milgi technique. The concentration of force in the lower abdomen or groin evokes the symbolism of that body part as the beginning and source of human life. It is widely believed amongst top athletes, sportsmen, and exercise physiologists that engaging in regular sexual intercourse during the course of training and preparation for a competition is more likely to have a negative effect on energy levels affecting one's focus, concentration, and aggressiveness. Certainly the ancient warriors had similar ideas, refraining from intercourse before battle to avoid the ultimate dissipation of ki energy from the danjun.

The poomsae line is horizontal and is consistent with the horizontal direction of guardian ki flow within the Belt Channel. This vessel is the only one of the eight extraordinary meridians that is aligned horizontally around the body. It wraps around the other channels like a belt to maintain protection against any negative energy from the external environment. The practice of the poomsae pyongwon may help to strengthen this protective ki field circling around the body.

The Belt Channel is said to involve seven distinct ki layers extending outward to form a protective field around the body, and each one corresponds to the seven energy centers arranged around the Thrusting Channel. The layer closest to the body is formed by the lowest energy center, while the outermost layer is supplied with ki from the highest energy center. It may be supplemented by fresh ki energy from heaven and earth.

This ki energy practice starts by moving the ki from the danjun to the navel and circling it through the left side to the Gate of Life point in the back .This point is on the same level but opposite to the navel, and from here it continues to circle forward through the right side to reach back to the navel. This is like tying a belt around the middle of the body. This corresponds to the abdominal energy center or danjun located along the axis of the Thrusting Channel. Its advanced practice involves three stages, starting from circling through a small arc around the core of the Thrusting Channel, to circling around the external body surface, and finally extending out at a distance through the external field that surrounds the body. This exercise may be repeated upward or downward at horizontal levels corresponding to the other six energy centers which are all located around the core of the Thrusting Channel. These include the Root, Solar Plexus, Heart, Throat, Third Eye, and Crown energy centers, and the martial artist can finally join the core, the surface, and the field layers together to form a complete protective cocoon.

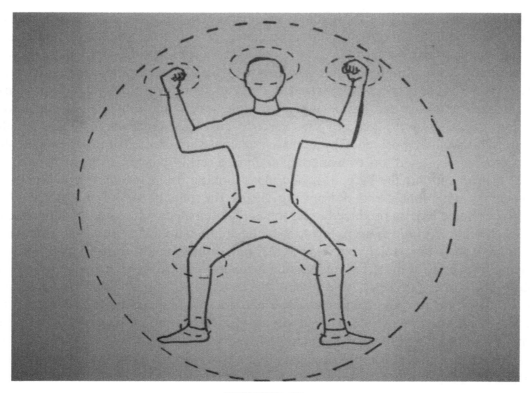

PICTURE 25
Protective Ki Energy from the Belt Channel

POOM EXERCISE NO. 60

Casual interpretation of Steps 1 and 2 shows how to escape from two opponents. The first man seizes you in a tight neck squeeze while the second one launches a strike from your left side. Force the first attacker's encircling arms apart to break his hold. Gouge his eyes and twist to your right side to unbalance him. Finish him off with a knife-hand strike to his neck pressure point as he falls. The technique of tong milgi or pushing hands develops the defensive ki field around the defender's throat while han sonnal area makki or single low section knife-hand block fortifies the protective ki shield around the defender's groin.

Steps 3 and 4 resemble the motions of a farmer armed with a sharp machete as he chops the overgrown bush on all sides, clearing the farmland in preparation for planting. The technique of palkup-ollyo-chigi in Step 5 mimics ancient dry farming rice planting techniques, where the farmer would walk behind his oxen ploughing the fields, throwing rice seeds over his shoulder into the freshly opened soil.

POOM EXERCISE NO. 61

Steps 3 through 6 show how the defendant would fight off the second attacker.

Intercept his lead hand with your open palm, trapping it. Counter-attack with your rising elbow strike to the opponent's chin. Then kick the attacker in the groin to immobilize him and grab him in both hands. Turn and swing your left leg upward between his thighs to execute a reaping throw. These kicks that challenge the practitioner's balance and composure may be likened to the swift leg lifting steps, acrobatic twists, and spins that are part of the choreography of the vigorous farmers' dance.

PICTURE 26
Acrobatic Farmers Nongak Dance Troupe

The internal energy practice of poomsae pyongwon uses han sonnal montong bakkat makki (single knife-hand mid-section outward block), followed by palkup ollyo chigi (elbow uppercut), ap chagi (front kick), and momdollyo yop chagi (turning side kick) to reinforce the defensive ki fields at the solar plexus, the Third Eye, the crown, and both knees and feet.

POOM EXERCISE NO. 62

Steps 6 through 8 bear some resemblance to the impressive sangmo dance, where long ribbons attached to the dancers' heads twirl up and down, spiraling through wide circles as the men leap about in their ecstatic performance. On the rice fields these movements would be akin to cutting the base of the mature rice stalks with a crescent-shaped sickle at harvest time. Kodureo-olgul-yop makki also resembles the farmer gathering the thick bales of rice stalk over his shoulder to the threshing area.

The following technique of dankyo-teok-jireugi in Step 9 appears to follow the whipping movements of the farmer slapping the rice stalks against the floor to separate the rice grains while clearing away the remaining chaff with his foot.

In the festival dance, this also takes the form of a dancer beating the special janggo drum's double surfaces with both hands while raising his leg momentarily in joyous expression. This drum is usually suspended from the neck of the player while he plays a percussion beat with two sticks. The right hand stick or yeolchae is made from light bamboo, giving a high pitch tone, while the left hand instrument or gungchae is a wooden-tipped mallet, making a soft, heavy sound from the female end of the drum.

Steps 6 through 8 reflect the defender's escape options against a double collar grab.

Seize his right hand with your left hand and strike the Yin vital point of his biceps with your right knife-hand. Sweep both arms upward in half-circles to clear his arms and apply an arm bar with your right hand against his triceps, forcing him to bend forward. Crank his trapped arm upward with both hands, forcing him to turn his back to you. Sweep him off his feet, knocking him to the ground and mount his back. Yank his collar backward and smash your fists into his temple (intersection of Yang meridians of large intestine and gall bladder). This sequence activates the cycle of destruction from the vital points of the pericardium (fire), large intestine (metal), and gall bladder (wood).

Step 7 is a method where the martial artist, by circling the hands overhead, can draw fresh heavenly ki energy into the arms in the technique of sonnal area makki (low section knife-hand block) to reinforce the lower half of the protective energy field. Likewise, in kodureo olgul yop makki (augmented high section side block) of Step 8, fresh protective ki from the earth is pulled upward to reinforce the upper half of the defender's defensive cocoon.

POOM EXERCISE NO. 63

Meongye-chigi or yoke strike performed in the crossed stance in Step 10 resembles a scarecrow in the fields, an important element to keep away voracious birds that can destroy the rice crop. It also bears close similarity to another member of the dance troupe beating a rhythm on the sogo drum. This small, flat drum is usually held in one hand and struck with a stick in the other.

This technique demonstrates how the defender can break free from a rear bear hug.

Drop your center of gravity to unbalance him. Then push both elbows out to the sides, breaking the encircling hold. This extends and strengthens the guardian ki field at the level of one's heart.

Steps 11 and 12 start with hecho-santeul makki and may represent the introduction of a third type of drum, the large, flat junggo drums. These are positioned on both sides of the performer, who plays both of them using the correct rhythm by beating each one using sticks held in both hands. Then keumgang makki is performed on the raised leg stance, evoking a white crane stepping through the ploughed fields, stalking insects disturbed by the hooves of the oxen. The dancer strikes both drums together then lifts his left hand high toward heaven, his right hand pointing to the earth, before pulling the right foot up to the opposite knee in the one-legged stance of the white crane.

POOM EXERCISE NO. 64

This latter sequence is a continuation from Steps 11 through 13 and includes Step 21.

The defender has escaped the rear bear hug and counter-attacks his assailant. Seize his wrists in both hands and thrust your head backward to butt his face. Toss the offender's arms over his head to spin him around his vertical axis. Then secure his arms behind his back and smash your knee up into his kidneys. Force him down with a side-kick to the back of his knee. Grab his head and finish him off with an elbow strike to the head.

Step 11 uses the hecho santeul makki (opening mountain block) to reinforce the defensive ki field around the Third Eye. Keumgang makki (diamond block) of Step 12 extends the ki field up and down to wrap around the defender.

TRANSPLANTING SONG

MEN: *O girl picking cotton in a dense field,*
I'll pick cotton and cotton ball for you,
So let's pledge a marriage bond.
O girl picking lotus leaves at Konggal Pond in Sangju,
I'll pick lotus seeds and wild rice for you,
So let's pledge a marriage bond.

WOMEN: *Where has the idle owner gone after planting seedlings?*
He left no trace but went to his concubine
Whose room is a flowerbed, while the wife's is a lotus pond.

NOTES

CHAPTER 13

SIPJIN POOMSAE

PICTURE 27
Sipjin Poomsae Symbol

Sipjin poomsae symbolizes the thought of 10 longevity of the sipjang saeng,
Two heavenly bodies and three natural resources,
Two plants and three animals ,
All add up to ten creatures of long life.
Sun, moon, mountain, water and stone,
Pine tree, herb of eternal youth, tortoise, deer and crane.
Multiplying with endless development and growth like the decimal system,
hundreds, thousands, millions and billions inside the heavenly garden.

In more modern times, the philosophy of the poomsae sipjin is seen in the miraculous transformation of South Korea from a poor, war-ravaged, Third World country into a wealthy industrialized nation able to punch above its weight in world affairs.

From the indignities suffered under subjugation by their Japanese masters in the early part of the twentieth century to the deprivations of the second World War when its citizens were forcibly conscripted by their powerful neighbor, to the ravages of the civil war that split their country soon after with the loss of millions of lives, the Korean people have demonstrated an indomitable will to survive.

The Five-Year Economic and Social Development Plan was authored by the military leader General Park Chung Hee in the 1960s, leading to the economic growth of the industrial sector also known as "the Miracle of the Han River," as well as the expansion of railways and other means of transportation. Coupled with the introduction of Taekwondo to the four corners of the world, South Korea's stature has been raised and its influence in world events and has enjoyed an infinite multiplication in only the last two decades.

The ten creatures of long life (namely sun, moon, mountain, water, stone, pine tree, herb of eternal youth, tortoise, deer, and crane) are to be found in the Korean version of the creation of the universe. These are the same objects and creatures that appear in the sipjang saeng, Korea's famous artistic mural which shows the breathtaking image of a heavenly garden floating in a heavenly lake. Included in the magnificent painting's background are serene-looking animals and birds.

PICTURE 28
Ten Symbols Of Longevity Depicted In Sipjang Saeng Mural

In the beginning, the world did not exist according to this myth. A deity named Yul-ryeo and a goddess named Mago appeared. Yul-ryeo subsequently died and Mago gave birth to two goddesses, Gung-hee and So-hee. They in turn each gave birth to two Men of Heaven and two Women of Heaven. After the birth of the heavenly people, Yul-ryeo was revived, and through him was created the heaven, the earth, and the oceans. Four elements were created including ki, fire, water, and the earth. The latter in turn mixed and gave rise to herbs and plants, birds and animals—the ten creatures of longevity.

Mago decided to stay with Yul-ryeo, whose body became the world, and the heavenly people ruled all living things from their heavenly abode named Magoseong in honor of the goddess. In the thought of ten longevity, these creatures carry special significance and importance to the lives of the Koreans. These objects and creatures are invested with the heavenly or cosmic energy called ki.

The sun is seen as a constant source of light in contrast to the moon, which is always changing. It is described as the light of heaven, giving and nourishing life. It is important in the process of photosynthesis, where plants produce and store energy which is transferred to animals and man to sustain life when eaten.

The fullness and brightness of the moon on the fifteenth day of the eight lunar month marks the end of the harvest and is celebrated by Koreans in the mid-autumn moon festival of Chuseok, with thanksgiving for a bountiful harvest, longevity, and family unity.

The mountains seem to maintain their shape forever while defending their surroundings, and water has been around since the creation of the world, symbolizing the flow of life and infinite flexibility in Taoist teaching. Without water, no human can live beyond a week.

Stone is the hardest and most enduring of things in nature and some of the Dolmen stone tombs found in the Korean peninsula date as far back as 3000 B.C. These weigh up to ten tons and have on their surfaces accurate maps of constellations around the North Star carved by the ancient Koreans. The cover-stone usually took the shape of a turtle's back, a creature revered for its longevity and the ancient people believed once dead, they would enjoy a long life in the afterworld.

PICTURE 29
Ancient Korean Dolmen Stone Tomb

Pine trees seem to live centuries, remaining evergreen even in the coldest winters, indicating their vitality and dignity. The red superior pine needle oil helps to build the blood and support the body's immune system against all kinds of parasites, viruses, bacteria, and fungi. The pine wood is lightweight but extremely strong, and it is used to build coffins that transport the spirits of the dead to the afterlife.

The ancient herb of eternal youth or Reishi mushroom is considered a vital ingredient in Korean medicine and is said to grow in the land of immortals, bringing eternal life to those who eat it.

The tortoise is famous for living for centuries, and possesses a tough shell exoskeleton attached to its ribs as protection. Its' shell has intricate carvings which have been used from ancient times for divination.

The white cranes showed above are considered companions of the Daoist immortals. The white crane is said to possess longevity because it knows how to conserve and protect its essence or postnatal ki, which is stored in the kidneys and circulates through the eight extraordinary vessels creating marrow and semen.

Deer are also considered companions to the Daoist immortals, and medicine made from their horns contain high concentrations of testosterone and insulin growth hormone to strengthen the bones and improve the bone marrow to increase human health and vitality.

BONE MARROW WASHING

The major theme of ki energy training in this poomsae follows the concept of bone marrow washing whereby the fatty yellow marrow is gradually replaced by the red marrow to enhance blood-producing capability. Advanced practitioners are also able to channel and store excess ki energy in the marrow, a process which also improves health and increases longevity. These methods include absorbing the external ki energy from the environment, which comes from the sun and moon, through the skin, muscles, and tissue into the bones. It also involves using the proper breathing techniques to direct and concentrate the ki from the breath inside the marrow, transforming it into red marrow in the process. The transformed bone is usually much heavier and stronger.

This is usually complemented by improving the intake and absorption of ki energy from healthy foods and nutritional supplements like extracts from deer horn, the Reishi mushroom, or the pine needle oil and teas. Thus this poomsae illustrates the external and internal methods that will result in the growth of the bones and multiplication of the red marrow.

The bone marrow, as the primary site of blood cell production, is also important in Taoist belief since the ki energy is said to be stored here as well. It is found in the long bones, including the femur and the humerus, the flat bones of the vertebral spine, the pelvis, the ribs, the sternum, the scapula, and the cranium. In adults, most of the bone marrow in the long bones is of the yellow type, which is mainly fat and doesn't produce any blood. Breathing practice coupled with ki energy storage is said to convert this marrow into the desirable red marrow which, by producing lymphocytes in addition to red blood cells and platelets, acts as a key component of the lymphatic system. This marrow transformation enhances the tensile strength and heaviness of the bones, which would be of particular interest to the martial artist.

The Chinese letter (+), meaning ten, is the form of the poomsae line, which is expressed in the symbol of a cross. It can signify an infinite numbering of the decimal system and ceaseless development of each of the four sides of the cross extending in horizontal and vertical planes to the ends of the universe. The vertical and horizontal lines meeting in the center may represent the fusion of the celestial and the earthly, the spiritual and the rational, the active and the passive, the positive and the negative, and the male and the female attributes respectively. Some religions and individuals make the sign of the cross, drawing on spiritual power from the Celestial or Supreme Being as protection from evil forces.

Sipjin may be interpreted as ten pearls of fighting wisdom. This poomsae conceals ten different methods of fortifying the body's weak spots, making the martial artist impregnable and able to survive and recover quickly from any attack. This forms the basis of the "iron shirt" training method.

POOM EXERCISE NO. 65

First Method

In Step 1 the defender demonstrates hwangso makki (bull block) in response to a double wrist grab.

Toss your arms upward like an angry bull rearing its horns. Then twist your wrists outward to break his grip.

This technique is also an important form of training to develop the "iron head" capability to shrug off powerful, crushing head blows with the same ease that a rutting male adult deer can establish its dominance in head-butting and antler clashing over a weaker rival. It takes the form of lifting slab objects of gradually increasing weights and smashing them down on the top of the head. Later on, without the aid of any object, the experienced practitioner may simply use the mind alone to channel Yang ki energy from the sun to fortify the same spot.

POOM EXERCISE NO. 66

Second and Third Methods

Steps 2 and 7 introduce sonbadak kodureo montong bakkat makki (palm augmented outward middle section block) response against a left wrist grab.

Weaken his grip by cranking your left hand to the side in a circular motion. Smash your right palm-heel against his forearm to damage his wrist.

POOM EXERCISE NO. 67

Pyonsokkeut upeo tzireugi (horizontal spear-hand thrust) in Steps 3 and 8 is another method. This is effective against a similar single-hand wrist grab.

Twist your left hand clockwise around his right hand to counter-grip his wrist. Thrust the tips of your right hand over your left forearm to prise off his right hand.

Internal energy training here involves using the mind to focus ki energy into the bones of the fingers, strengthening them immensely for "iron finger" strikes. This is achieved by directing the external ki energy from the Work Palace point in the center of the right palm into the bones of the left forearm and channeling it into the fingertips of the left hand while sliding the right hand slowly over the left forearm. The same process is performed to strengthen the fingers of the right hand. The practitioner may also condition and fortify the fingertips by gripping the open end of a large sack in one hand while repeatedly thrusting the open palm into the peas contained inside, later on increasing the level of difficulty by replacing the peas with small metal balls or pebbles and finally fine sand.

POOM EXERCISE NO. 68

Fourth Method

This technique is used to fortify the eyes and enable the defender to withstand heavy blows to these weak spots without injury. Initially, training involves tying a cord made from weak breakable fiber material loosely around the head and jerking hard with both hands, pulling outward to snap the cord. Later on the practitioner may use the mind alone to channel the ki energy to the eyes. This technique is performed with the practitioner in a stable balanced horseback stance evocative of the rooted fixture of an immovable mountain.

POOM EXERCISE NO. 69

Fifth Method

Steps 4 and 5 involve the defense against a neck choke from the front.

Squeeze the Yang vital point LI (4) of the large intestine meridian in both hands to break his grip and force his hands off to either side. Step under his right arm, pulling him forward, and strike the Yin vital point of the heart meridian inside his armpit.

This attack alternates vital point strike using the Yang and Yin principle.

The weak point of the throat is the next target of this "iron shirt" practice. Just as in the previous example, initial training involves tying a cord made from stronger but breakable fiber material loosely around the neck and jerking hard with both hands, pulling outward to snap the cord. Later on the practitioner may use the mind alone to channel the external ki energy to the throat. A significant part of the power created is derived from the stability of the horseback stance.

POOM EXERCISE NO. 70

Sixth Method

Bawi milgi (boulder pushing) technique in Step 15 shows the defender how to break free from an attacker who grabs his hands. This may be similar to an angry crane bumping and buffeting its adversary with its body and powerful wings.

Twist to the left side, bumping and unbalancing the aggressor. Step forward, pushing your hands out in a circular motion to break his grip.

In this technique, the practitioner imagines that he is drawing on external ki energy into both hands from the heavy cover of the Dolmen stone tomb as he raises it carefully into place. This helps to develop "iron palm" strength in both hands.

POOM EXERCISE NO. 71

Seventh Method

In Step 16, the technique of sonnaldeung montong hecho makki (ridge-hand middle section opening block) can be used to escape from a double grip. In this scenario, the opponent faces you, gripping your wrists in his hands.

Drop your weight low into a horseback stance, pulling him off balance. Swing both hands upward, crossing your midline in half-circles to weaken his hold. Then spread them downward, freeing both wrists from his grasp.

This is also a method of developing "iron crotch" capability to withstand any strike to the groin in men. The practitioner starts by sitting in the horseback stance with a heavy weight attached to his genitals. By squeezing both hands into fists to generate tension, he lifts the heavy object using his genitals alone. With further practice he is able to lift objects in excess of 100 pounds. Advanced practitioners may be able to use the mind alone to channel external ki energy down to fortify the groin against the most powerful kicks without injury. This is a demonstration of the white crane's famed ability to guard its essence stored in the kidneys to ensure longevity. The moon as a symbol of creation balances and harmonizes the power of the sun to endow the practitioner with Yin energy, generating longevity and fertility.

POOM EXERCISE NO. 72

Eight and Ninth Methods

The technique of chettari-jireugi (fork-shape simultaneous punch) in Step 21 is effective against an opponent who grabs your wrists in a double grip.

Draw your hands downward to your left hip, pulling your attacker off balance. Strike him in the groin with your front kick. Then thrust your hands forward at chest level to break his hold.

The practitioner fortifies the left and right sides of the abdomen sequentially by smashing heavy Chinese kettles held in both hands into his body. In advanced "iron shirt "practice, the mind alone is used to channel the external ki energy to fortify both sides of the abdomen to protect the internal organs.

POOM EXERCISE NO. 73

Tenth Method

The final technique of sonnal deung montong makki (ridge-hand middle section block) shows an appropriate response to a double wrist grab in Steps 27 and 28.

Drop into a left back stance, pulling your hands to your left hip to unbalance the opponent. Twist your right wrist out to the side in a half-circle to break free from his left hand. Simultaneously, swing your left hand toward your right elbow to escape from his right hand.

In this final phase of "iron shirt" training, the practitioner fortifies the weak spots of the solar plexus and floating ribs by smashing heavy wooden or metal posts held in both hands into these vital parts. Similarly advanced "iron shirt" practice uses the mind alone to channel the external ki energy to fortify the solar plexus and floating ribs. This develops the impregnable "iron ribs" similar to the hard shell or exoskeleton of the tortoise, which is attached to its ribs as protection from its enemies.

POOM EXERCISE NO. 74

This poomsae employs some characteristic traits from the white crane method. This is evident in the following sequences, like in Steps 4 and 5 where the defender executes hecho santeul makki (opening mountain block) against a stick-wielding opponent.

After absorbing the force of the blow with both hands, the defender grabs the weapon. Then he pulls the opponent forward into a crippling blow aimed inside his armpit.

POOM EXERCISE NO. 75

Another example of the white crane method is found in Steps 26 through 28 where the defender uses the sonnal deung montong makki (ridge-hand middle section block) to rush out his hands to parry away the attacker's punch with his reverse ridge-hand. The other palm is positioned face down close to the opponent to ward off his other limb or strike his lower section with the fingertips. This creates an opening by exposing the attacker's chest, which is quickly exploited with chettari-jireugi (double simultaneous punch) to his chest to blast him away.

The poomsae line of sipjin as represented by the + sign resembles the development of the rail lines that initially ran from the south of the peninsula to the north to join the Trans-Siberian Railway, particularly the Gyeongi Line from Seoul through Kaesong, and Pyongyang to Shinuiji on the border with China. This rail line was abruptly severed in 1948 by the Demilitarized Zone (DMZ) or line that was created to separate both north and south and maintain world peace. This zone was the consequence of World War II, with the two great armies of the Soviet Union and the Allied military forces facing each other across the buffer zone of the line of the 38th parallel and agreeing on an armistice that cooled down the hostilities of the brutal.

Many Koreans hope that one day, when both countries are no longer officially at war, this rail line will lead all the way to Europe by joining with the Trans-Siberian Rail Lines just like the silk trade route of earlier centuries. However, informal skirmishes have occurred regularly since the cessation of overt hostilities, such as the invasion of South Korean territory through tunnels dug under the DMZ from North Korea. These were discovered from 1974 to 1990, numbering seventeen in all, tunneling under the most militarized border in the world, and some were large enough to permit 2,000 North Korean soldiers to cross within an hour.

Bawi milgi or rock pushing seems to symbolize the hard work and tears of the Korean worker shed when clearing up the hard terrain to lay kilometers of fresh rail lines for the expansion of transportation and industry. It also bears some resemblance to the shifting of a large boulder to open a tunnel and allow escapees from the north to glimpse the reassuring rays of sunshine and freedom. This narration of events seems to be made out in Steps 19 through 24.

POOM EXERCISE NO. 76

Imagine a Korean trapped on the northern side of the DMZ long after the cessation of hostilities has devised an escape plan. On the appointed day, he makes his way close to the border with the south, taking care to evade the border guards posted along the way. Then he locates the tunnel's entrance as expected and crawls through its dark, long, narrow corridor cut through the DMZ like several who have made the same journey through the secret passage. His head scrapes against the makeshift door guarding the exit at the other end, bringing the realization that he has almost reached freedom in the south.

He pushes aside the metal bolt to open the door and rolls away the boulder blocking the final exit into the open. Something has gone wrong in his plans, though, and a border guard waits in ambush. He is armed with a loaded rifle and fixed bayonet. As the refugee steps out into the open air of freedom, the armed guard jumps upon him, intending to run his sharp blade through his side. Instinctively, the refugee sucks in his stomach and the blade barely misses. He shifts to one side, knocking the gun barrel away with his left hand. Then both are locked in a fierce struggle to possess the rifle. The escapee pulls the guard forward, off balance, and aims a hard kick into his unprotected groin. The border guard continues to hang onto the weapon as the escapee struggles to disarm him. He kicks him repeatedly into submission and finishes the soldier off with a powerful elbow smash to the back of his head.

There is no time to waste as the border guard crumples unconsciously to the ground. He quickly rolls back the boulder to block the exit to the tunnel and turns away to his new destiny. A few minutes have been lost in this unexpected life and death struggle, and according to his calculations he is still on track to meet up with the contact in the new land.

"Yesterday a Thousand Soldiers"
Yesterday a thousand soldiers passed down the village street,
Going to war, going perhaps to die.
Many of them glanced at my silken gown.
Many of them smiled because I smiled.
But only one knew of my hidden tears.

– Anonymous

NOTES

CHAPTER 14

JITAE POOMSAE

PICTURE 30
Jitae Poomsae Symbol

A man standing on the earth and looking towards the heaven,
Gathering energy to spring upwards,
Which is the meaning of Jitae poomsae.
Gathering the energy force of the earth up into strong muscles,
And after the jump the energy returns to the earth.
All living things come from and return to the earth,
This symbolizes the principle of Jitae poomsae.

The Poomsae Jitae represents the concept of earth power. Koreans believe that apart from living organisms, even inanimate objects are filled with ki force that can be tapped into and subsequently released, like a geyser springing forth from the center of the earth, or the belching of clouds of toxic fumes and tons of ash from an erupting volcano. Another example is the immense rumbling forces generated by an earthquake. Examples of the power of the earth in the form of devastating earthquakes have been recorded in history.

In the annals of China, the 1556 Jiajing Great Earthquake was described in this account after taking 830,000 lives: "In the winter of 1556, an earthquake catastrophe occurred in the Shaanxi and Shanxi Provinces. In our Hua County, various misfortunes took place. Mountains and rivers changed places and roads were destroyed. In some places, the ground suddenly rose up and formed new hills, or it sank abruptly and became new valleys. In other areas a stream burst out in an instant, or the ground broke and new gullies formed. Huts, official houses, temples, and city walls collapsed all of a sudden."

Descriptions of the effects of the A.D. 358 Nicomedia (Imzit, Turkey) earthquake by Ammianus Marcellinus, a fourth century writer read "...at the same time fearful earthquakes shattered numerous cities and mountains throughout Asia, Macedonia, and Pontus with repeated shocks. Now pre-eminent among the instances of manifold disaster was the collapse of Nicomedia, the metropolis of Bithynia, and I shall give a true and concise account of the misfortune of its destruction.

"On the 24th of August, at the first break of day, a terrific earthquake utterly destroyed the city and its suburbs. And since most of the houses were carried down the slopes of the hills, they fell one upon another, while everything resounded with the vast roar of their destruction. Meanwhile the hill tops re-echoed with all manner of outcries, of those seeking their wives, their children, and their relatives. Finally after the second hour, but well before the third, the air which was now bright and clear, revealed the fatal ravages that lay concealed..."

When performing Jitae poomsae the feet should be firmly rooted by gripping the ground with the outside toes. Try to imagine a chameleon glued strongly to a tree branch by its feet, defeating your concerted efforts to pry it off. To enhance the flow of the earth power, it is advised that the practitioner engage in the reverse Taoist breathing pattern from this moment onward. This means using the danjun, waist, and legs to release this force while keeping the mind focused on where it is going.

Visualize your body sinking slowly, lowering your center of gravity until the ki energy in your danjun descends downward, making connection with the ground. Thus the upper body is empty and the lower body is full and rooted to the ground and can link up with the earth's energy and reflect back up into your body.

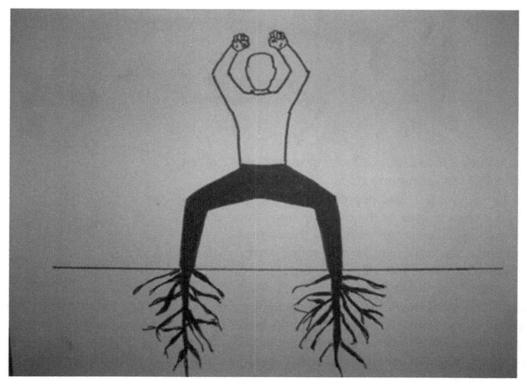

PICTURE 31
Connecting Powerful Earth Energy To Rooted Horse Back Stance

The waist is very important, as it releases a tremendous amount of ki from the danjun and transfers the rooting power from the earth and legs to the upper body. Propel the spiraling energy wave from the ground through your legs, magnifying it with movement of the waist and coupled with the opening and closing of the spine. The center of gravity must remain at a constant height above the ground, as one moves with the centrifugal force of the waist and a twist causes the arms to strike outward with great power. Make this an energy wave rippling up from the ground through your hands and deep into your opponent.

When a blow is struck with the fist it is akin to a huge force thrown upward, starting from below the soles of the feet and spiraling upward, uniting the upper and lower body, incorporating every muscle in the body rather than using the limited power of the shoulders. Each movement starts in the feet, ascending upward through the legs, rotating the waist, the ribcage, and shoulders, then the arms to end in the hands. Immense energy can be initiated with the whole body connected and moving as one, opening and closing in an instant just like when you sneeze. It is important that the whole body be relaxed to lessen tension which may obstruct energy flow into the limbs. In simpler terms, each part of the body is attached to and moved by a part that moved just before.

To ensure proper technique, it is important to avoid pushing upon impact, which bounces your force back. Rather, the martial artist should focus on using the mental intent rather than the fist to pierce through the opponent.

Also resist cocking and tensing your pelvis and shoulders, or creating an obvious wind-up followed by a large forward lunge. Utilize smooth flowing power with a small movement, allowing the release of earth power to pull your forward step.

This is the application of the Eastern theory of internal power that advances a step further compared to the more orthodox Western formula of external power, which simply describes force as equal to mass multiplied by acceleration. Conventional science assumes that a small-bodied man or woman has no hope of developing phenomenal power in their technique unless they are blessed with blinding superhuman speed to compensate for the obvious disadvantage of their small mass. And as one advances in age, the older and slower martial artist is at a great disadvantage when pitted in a fight with a much younger attacker. However, there are many instances of aging martial artists who are past their peak successfully defending themselves against younger bullies. Similarly, small-bodied martial artists have been able to prevail against bigger and stronger opponents. In fact, most Asian fighting arts are based on the principle of a smaller person being able to overcome a much bigger and more aggressive adversary. This is based on the reality of an unprovoked fight where you may not always be the bigger or stronger fighter.

Many steps of Poomsae Jitae are practiced slowly, especially the rising hand movements which are conducive for ki to flow in a healing way. Its smooth and flowing motion balances the ki circulation, removing all blockages. Once there is connection of the upper and lower body, ki saturates the individual, soothing and creating a state of well-being and calm.

The practitioner should visualize the tremendous ki rising like a geyser from the danjun and streaming like a great river around the body as it roars up and down around the arms and legs. This tidal wave of ki vibrates throughout to unblock the blockages in the meridians and vessels, making the body healthy. To enter this phase of active meditation the practitioner should be completely relaxed mentally and physically, without any tension in the mind and body. Every joint must be open and muscle relaxed to lower the center of gravity, and there is no thought as the ki circulates effortlessly through the body.

Rooting also permits one's ki to flow and connect with nature, in order to harness the energy coming from the earth. This earth energy flows everywhere and penetrates every surface and pore in the body, enveloping the whole body from the inside out to connect the spirit to the body. This creates an interaction that awakens one to a deeper level of perception and intuition, making one able to sense the energy from others and channel ki energy through one's self to heal others.

In every step in the poomsae the Taekwondo practitioner strives to remain rooted to the ground, maintaining a balanced stance in order to unleash the earth's energy that arises from below. The following examples illustrate this principle.

The junbi seogi is used to direct the ki energy from the danjun through the perineum into the lower limbs during exhalation. From here the ki passes through the bone structure and joints of the legs into the Bubbling Well spot in the soles of the feet and deep into the earth like two bolts being screwed into the ground.

The practice of Poomsae Jitae involves teaching the practitioner to redirect the pushing or striking force from an assailant into the rooting force, sinking it into the ground without losing balance. This requires the maintenance of proper spinal posture and relaxation of the joints and muscles to sink the opponent's negative energy into the earth. Subsequently, this energy is sucked back up, augmented with powerful earth energy with the inhalation, and passed upward through the muscle and bone structure of the legs to store in the danjun. Thus one can absorb the opponent's negative ki and neutralize it in the earth before storing it within the danjun.

POOM EXERCISE NO. 77

Steps 1 through 4 are performed at a reduced speed in a sequence involving montong bakkat makki (outward middle block) in the back stance before switching to olgul makki (high section block) and montong baro jireugi (reverse hand punch) in the front stance, gripping the ground with the toes.

The practical application of this principle is realized when the attacker grabs the defender's collar in his right hand in preparation for a strike. Squeeze the Third Space vital point in the back of the attacker's hand to loosen his grip. Twist his arm counterclockwise over his shoulder, forcing him to turn his back to you. Thrust your right forearm against his elbow, forcing it to point upward. Push your left hand up his back to immobilize him in a combined shoulder and wrist lock.

Kingsley Umoh

The upward movement of the high block is similar to the floating technique of the flying crane style. During the performance of this sequence, the martial artist switches from a back stance into a front low stance, planting both feet firmly into the ground. The practitioner should visualize the opponent's force being absorbed by his body and transferred into the earth through his rooted stance. By forming a fist and raising the arm slowly into a high block, one summons the ki power back from the earth into the upper body and hands, visualizing it flowing up his legs, through his pelvis and his spine, surging upward into his arms as an overwhelming tsunami-like force. As the ki flows into the upper body, the martial artist is able to uproot his feet and transition easily from a back stance into a front stance before replanting them, a move closely related to the white crane attacking technique of spitting.

POOM EXERCISE NO. 78

The following sequences of Steps 5 through 7 employ the similar principle of transfer of energy from a rooted stance into the opponent's vital areas.

Step forwards and block the opponent's kick with your left fore-arm. Intercept his punch with your left palm and counter with a swift groin kick. Then apply an arm bar on his captured arm, forcing him to the ground.

The low block, arae makki, is used to channel the ki into the earth in the rooted front stance. Han sonnal makki (single knife-hand) is used to absorb an opponent's incoming blow and sink the force into the earth, rooting with the back stance, a technique similar to swallowing in Fukienese White Crane, where "four ounces is used to topple 1,000 pounds."

After absorbing the assailant's attack, one follows up using the white crane's spitting tactic of a forward attack with a high kick. The emphasis is on uprooting the stance without losing balance in preparation for the kick, then rooting the stance back into the ground.

POOM EXERCISE NO. 79

Steps 8 and 9 are the defender's response to a shirt collar grab like in Step 1.

Squeeze the Third Space vital point on the back of opponent's left hand to break the hold. Kick his groin to knock him down . Then apply an arm bar on his captured arm, forcing him to the ground.

This is another example of ki channeling downward when the montong bakkat makki (outward middle block) absorbs the opponent's force and directs it downward through the rooted back stance. Then the ki is sucked upward and the stance uprooted to facilitate a high kick and a forward step.

POOM EXERCISE NO. 80

Steps 10 through 12 explore the same kind of response to a double collar grab.

Squeeze the Third Space vital point on the back of opponent's right hand to break his grip. Push his right hand upward with your left hand to free your collar. Break his remaining grip by deflecting his left arm upward to expose his armpit. Punch his solar plexus simultaneously and finish him with double fist strikes to the head. The penultimate step is demonstrated by the keumgang montong jireugi (diamond front punch).

Again, just as in the previous steps, the martial artist switches into a front low stance, planting both feet firmly into the ground and raising the arm slowly into a high block to absorb the opponent's force through his structure, dissipating it inside the earth. This also bears some semblance to the white crane tactic of lifting with one hand to intercept an opponent's blow while simultaneously throwing a punch with the other.

POOM EXERCISE NO. 81

The sequence of Steps 15 through 24 illustrates how to overcome two attackers who have seized you at either hand.

Sink your weight and wrench both hands upward out of their grip, breaking free. Then swing your hand down to the left, smashing the Yin vital point intersection of the spleen and kidney meridians in the groin of the first opponent. Turn your attention to the second man and strike the Yin vital point of the liver meridian in his neck with your right knife-hand. Next, grab his head and smash your left hammer-fist into his temple (intersection of the Yang meridians of large intestine and gall bladder). Pull his hand towards your left hip and thrust your right heel down to break his ribs.

As before, the martial artist sinks his ki downward to connect with the earth's force, planting both feet firmly into the ground using the side horse stance. By thrusting both arms upward in the bull block, he imagines himself absorbing the adversary's ki power into his arms and dissipating it into the earth.

In the crane stance, the defender balances only on one foot and finds it necessary to channel the ki energy downward to root his stance. By linking the opponent's incoming force applied on his right hand with his left leg he is able to dissipate this energy into the earth without losing his balance. Similarly, by switching rapidly from a left foot to a right foot crane stance, this easily results in many martial artists becoming unbalanced. Again, arae makki is utilized by the practitioner to channel ki energy to his rooted right leg before performing the powerful side kick.

POOM EXERCISE NO. 82

Turn your attention back to the first attacker on your left side and seize his left arm . Pull his arm across to your right hip and thrust your left heel on the Yang vital point of the stomach meridian in the front of his knee joint. Punch the Yang vital point of the gall bladder meridian in his left side . Once he is knocked backward, strike again into his exposed armpit attacking the Yin vital point of the heart meridian to knock him out.

The attack sequence activates vital points of both Yang and Yin channels.

MEETING A PRIEST ON A MOUNTAIN BRIDGE

On a bridge below the Water Gate
I saw his shadow lying aslant the stones.
Amidst a thousand flickering leaves
How still he seemed!
I asked him what he sought among these mountains.
He answered not but pointed with his lifted staff
To formless clouds beyond the farthest peak.

NOTES

_____

_____

_____

_____

_____

_____

_____

_____

_____

_____

_____

_____

CHAPTER 15

CHONKWON POOMSAE

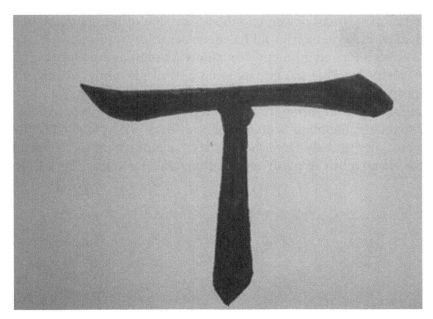

PICTURE 32
Chonkwon Poomsae Symbol

Large arm actions and gentle curves,
Show the greatness of Chonkwon thought.
Like Hwanin the heavenly king,
Submitting to the will of the Heaven,
Endowed with power by the Heaven,
And rising to worship the Heaven,
Soaring like an eagle toward the sky.
That is the principle of Chonkwon poomsae.

Another reference to the myth of origin of the Korean people is made again in the philosophy of this poomsae. Over 9,000 years ago, the progenitor of the Korean people, "Hwanin," was called the heavenly king. He settled down in the "heavenly" town as the capital near the heavenly sea and heavenly mountain, where the Han people as the heavenly race gave birth to the proper thought and actions from which Taekwondo was originated. The Han people here are the Koreans who mainly settled near the banks of the Han River rather the major Chinese ethnic group.

The Poomsae Chonkwon is based on such sublime history and thoughts. The ancient Koreans had also bestowed the role of religious minister or shaman on their kings and thus Hwanin may rightly be considered the first "heavenly king" or shaman king rather than his son Dangun, having obtained his divine rights to rule after coming down from the heaven, submitting to the will of Heaven, being endowed power by Heaven, and worshiping Heaven, which means the oneness between Heaven and a human being.

Motions in Poomsae Chonkwon are reminiscent of an eagle flying off toward the high sky. According to ancient Korean beliefs, some of which have persisted till modern times, the soul of the shaman does not ascend to the heavens or spiritual world, but rather spirits are invited to enter the shaman's body to enable him receive important secrets to help needy members of the community or perform such important functions as conveying the spirit of its dead members to heaven in a Nuk Kut ritual ceremony. The eagle has always been regarded as a symbol of spiritual power, and the possession of the shaman's body by a spirit in certain ritual dances is described as if the person's soul has been seized by an eagle.

The eagle has always been looked at in envy by all civilization as a majestic bird soaring to the highest heights in the heavens, easily ignoring the gravitational pull of the earth with the strokes of its immensely strong wings. It possesses a large hooked beak for tearing the flesh from its victims, and specializes in diving from a great height, using its strong, muscular legs to strike from above, sinking its powerful talons into the prey. Then its soars off, flapping its huge wings with its prize clutched in its tight grip. Usually the unfortunate animal or bird dies quickly from the shock emanating from the sudden brutality of the attack. Amongst all birds it has no equal in strength and is often considered the king of the skies. Men have tried

PICTURE 33
Majestic Eagle Swooping Down

to emulate this divine and powerful bird by attaching props of feathers to their arms, attempting to launch themselves unsuccessfully into the air.

In China and other parts of Asia, schools of fighting have studied the graceful and powerful movements of this enduring bird of prey, incorporating them into different principles of devastating attack and defensive tactics. These have been formulated into the following tactics emphasizing brutal and fierce strikes and crushing joint locks. They include precision strikes to the pressure points and soft targets like the eyes, throat, and areas of loose skin; attacking with a claw or striking with slicing action of powerfully conditioned fingers; and catching the head or limbs and seizing and ripping apart the joints, tendons, and pressure points.

The specialist in the eagle claw technique would also be proficient in attacks to the neck to shut down the throat and stop the breathing, locking the joints and legs, wrapping like a vine to hook the leg or elbow to attack the wrist or ankles, performing acrobatic aerial maneuvers for attack and defensive strikes, and being able to throw or reverse the opponent's grab. It has been said that the evidence of strikes received from one versed in these techniques are usually quite visible as multiple skin bruises, deep tissue bleeding and swellings, ripped throats or scrotums, as well as dislocated joints. The hallmark of this method is the powerful eagle claw, which relies on a speed and power combination and resembles the swift motion of simultaneously snatching and crushing an apple caught in mid-air in one's hooked fingers as it is thrown.

It starts with the open palm striking with lightning speed at the target, and then suddenly snapping and curling the fingers at the last moment just before contact to maximize damage. It also requires special training to strengthen the fingers into white-hot talons of steel capable of tearing flesh and tendons, and separating muscle from bone and causing intense pain.

The poomsae line reveals the rising of ki energy from its base like an eagle soaring up into the sky. This is an indirect reference to the transportation of the energy from the sexual organs rising upward through the sacrum and spinal cord to nourish the heavenly center in the brain, which is used to open the Third Eye or is ultimately transformed into ki energy to be circulated within the small heavenly circle. Poomsae Chonkwon also deals with the methods of separation of orgasm from ejaculation to conserve and control the transformation of the sexual ki energy inherent in each individual. This is necessary preparation for the development and opening of the Small Heavenly Circle as training progresses.

Taoist literature describes the transformation of this sexual energy into powerful spiritual essence once it has reached the brain. It also incorporates the belief that the danjun exists just below the umbilicus in front of the sacrum and serves as the main storage area of the ki energy. It may take up to three years of regular practice to fully open the Small Heavenly Circle. Celibacy is essential to accumulate a sufficient quantity of ki energy and increase longevity and health.

The Taoists believe in the conservation of vital bodily fluids to promote optimal human health including the avoidance of loss of seminal fluid, which is believed to store the most prenatal ki energy. This is mainly achieved through the practice of celibacy or the separation of the impulses of orgasm from ejaculation when engaged in sexual intercourse. Loss of sexual essence is believed to result in premature aging, poor health, and decreased longevity.

The following recommendations on ejaculation frequency based on a man's age were made in the Chinese text "Classic of the Plain Girl":

At age 20: Twice per day (good health) and once per day (poor health).
At age 30: Once per day (good health) and every other day (poor health).
At age 40: Every three days (good health) and every four days (poor health).
At age 50: Every five days (good health) and every ten days (poor health).
At age 60: Every ten days (good health) and every twenty days (poor health).
At age 70: Every thirty days (good health) and never (poor health).

PICTURE 34
Raising Sexual Ki Energy To The Brain

By training the muscles of the pelvis using special exercises, the aim is to separate orgasm from ejaculation in the man, resulting ultimately in greater enlightenment and even immortality. In the woman, on the other hand, the vital female essence is mainly lost in the form of menstruation and childbirth, and similar exercises to strengthen the vaginal and anal muscles may result in the conservation of blood flow or a cessation of menstruation.

Other benefits from these exercises include the treatment of impotence and premature ejaculation in men, as well as anorgasmia, frigidity, and menstrual problems in women. These Taoist methods when used in the union of a married couple are said to heighten the sexual pleasures into total bodily rather than genital orgasm, promoting greater fulfilling love between them while unifying and balancing the opposite sexual ki energies of each partner.

In comparison to feminine sexuality, men are considered the weaker element. By delaying or preventing ejaculation, the man is able to prolong the sexual contact and absorb the superior vitality inherent in the woman's female essence to strengthen his vitality.

Sexuality was an important part of the lives of the ancient Koreans such that it was commemorated privately in the form of erotic bronze coins depicting carved images of different sexual positions. These coins were usually given as gifts to young newlywed couples and were meant to educate them on the different forms of the sexual act and as a reminder of their sacred duty in the conception of children for the continuity of the family.

PICTURE 35
Ancient Korean Erotic Bronze Coins

CANON OF TAOIST WISDOM

(Collected by Emperor Tang)

...if a man has intercourse once without spilling his seed, his vital essence is strengthened.
If he does this twice, his hearing and vision are made clear.
If three times, all his physical illness will disappear.
The fourth time, he will begin to feel inner peace.
The fifth time, his blood will circulate powerfully.
The sixth time, his genitals will gain new prowess.
By the seventh, his thighs and buttocks will become firm.
The eighth time, his entire body will radiate good health.
The ninth time, his lifespan will be increased...

POOM EXERCISE NO. 83

The defender is faced with aggression from an opponent who grabs his collar in both hands.

Squeeze with your thumbs the Dorsal Center vital points located in the back of his hands. Then break his hold using nalgae-pyogi technique or wing-spreading posture.

Nalgae-pyogi also involves drawing up the ki energy from the root center to the heart energy center, which is primarily concerned with love relationships and the spirit according to Taoist beliefs. It may also be recognized as one of the initial steps in the act of intercourse when each partner undresses the other. As a more advanced Taoist practice, it represents the transformation of the sexual ki energy and raising it as the spirit form from the abode inside the sacrum up the spinal canal located in the center of the spine in stages using the mind and special breathing techniques. Here the ki energy is directed from the lower danjun to the middle danjun located in the solar plexus and extended into both palms.

POOM EXERCISE NO. 84

The characteristics of movements are large actions and arm actions forming gentle curves, thus symbolizing the greatness of Chonkwon thought. This explains the basis of fighting with sweeping arm action to clear the opponent's center line in preparation for a crushing attack to the exposed soft tissues as epitomized in the jumbi seogi and Steps 1 and 2.

The kyopson jumbi seogi or overlapping hands starts in front of the sacral plexus or root chakra as the practitioner summons ki energy using reverse abdominal respiration into the hands or "heavenly fists." Chonkwon's techniques are heavily dependent on powerful hand strikes, hence the need to direct ki to the upper limbs. The kyopson jumbi seogi is also a Taoist method of scrotal compression where the practitioner swallows ki energy in the breath and forces it downward in stages, passing it through the stomach, the danjun, and the groin to strengthen the scrotal sac and root center.

The sweeping, large circular wing action of both arms in Step 1 evokes the powerful upstrokes of a soaring eagle and is used by the defender to break the double grip of an adversary from his throat. His arms are swept apart to expose his center line and penetrate his defenses.

The upward sweeping arm movements indicate the flow of the sexual ki energy from the sexual organs through the spinal cord to the brain. By concentrating on using the expired breath and squeezing the pubo-coccygeus muscle of the perineum, the practitioner is able to suck the ki energy from the testicles or ovaries and force it through the perineum and up the spine in stages to nourish the upper danjun in the brain. The techniques involved are referred to as Testicular Breathing and Power Lock, and are utilized to propel the ki upward in concert with the Cranio-Sacral Pump, which utilizes the rearward movement of the sacrum, minor expansion and contraction of the cranial bones and sutures, tucking in of the chin, clenching of the jaw, and contracting of the muscles on the back of the neck to straighten the spine and propel the ki upward.

Thus the primordial and sexual energies are converted to ki, which is then transformed into the spirit energy. The spirit energy passes with the cerebrospinal fluid (CSF) through the central canal of the spinal cord to reach the fourth ventricle of the medulla and finally the Third Eye energy center located within the third ventricle of the mid-brain. Here it makes the pineal gland and pituitary gland vibrate in harmony, resulting in the fusion of the Um energy of the pineal gland with the Yang energy of the pituitary gland and the opening of the Third Eye. As the Third Eye opens it is able to receive cosmic energy which is directed inside the triangular space formed by the open palms held high above the head.

This cosmic ki energy is focused in the midline forehead between both eyebrows as the practitioner gazes upward through the hands…as a man looks upward toward the sky. The cosmic ki energy is absorbed and penetrates the front of the brain to reach the upper danjun located in the center. From here, this cosmic energy will descend and combine with the spirit energy inside the Third Eye, raising the consciousness further and resulting in the spiritual awakening and enlightenment of the practitioner.

POOM EXERCISE NO. 85

Step back into a right cat stance crouch, pulling the attacker off balance. Strike and grip his neck on each side with both deadly claw hands. Rip the carotid arteries with bam-jumeok-sosum jireugi (double knuckle uppercut strike).

One of the most distressing male sexual problems is that of premature ejaculation, where the male experiences orgasm and releases his seminal fluid within seconds after penetration, resulting in a frustrating and unfulfilling sexual act for the woman. The Taoists have taught different methods to relieve this problem which include the cessation of pelvic thrusting and partial withdrawal of the male organ to calm the fires of excitement. At the same time, the man curls the fingers of both hands inward and tightens his whole body, including the muscles of the perineum, until the level of sexual arousal decreases from its highest point. Usually with an understanding sexual partner, the man is able to resume thrusting at a slower pace, allowing the couple to enjoy a more fulfilling intercourse.

POOM EXERCISE NO. 86

In the following sequence of Steps 3 through 8, there is a repetition of the basic theme involving a twisting front stance with the trunk facing forward at an angle of forty-five degrees with the heel raised and the rear foot turned inward to evade an opponent's strike. This also mimics the crouching, dodging, and shifting movements of an alert raptor as it side-steps and readies to attack or defend itself from a different angle.

Lash out with hansonnal bitureo makki (single knife-hand twist block) to the enemy's biceps. Snap into a powerful eagle claw at the last moment. Swing downward to rip the opponent's arm muscles and tendons from the bone. Then pull him forward and strike the exposed Yin vital point of the heart meridian in his armpit. Break his joint with a side kick to the Yang vital point of the stomach meridian in front of his knee. Force him to the ground and apply an arm bar on his left arm.

The Yang and Yin principle is used when attacking targets above and below the waist.

These steps also illustrate an advanced Taoist sexual practice with the woman lying on her side. The man sweeps her top leg to one side, clutching and spreading her thighs as wide as possible. Then he pushes himself slowly inside her, alternating between deep and shallow thrusts. He makes nine superficial penetrations followed by one deep penetration, then eight shallow and two deep penetrations, then seven light and three deep penetrations, reaching one shallow and nine deep penetrations before reversing the sequence until he gets back to nine light and one deep penetration or until she reaches orgasm. This position helps remedy erection problems and anorgasmia in the woman. If there is no loss of seminal fluid in this position, it is said that the man's vigor will be multiplied a hundredfold.

When fighting off an adversary, the eagle will attack fiercely, buffeting and distracting it with its huge wingspan before stabbing at it with its powerful legs and talons. It also evokes similar movements of a ritual dance as the shaman possessed with the raptor's good spirit in ancient times would twirl and turn, twisting a white scarf while cleansing an individual possessed by a bad spirit.

POOM EXERCISE NO. 87

Steps 10 through 12 follow similar tactics when the defender's arm is seized. The blocks are made in a circular motion in order to deflect and control the opponent's strike. They are most effective when used as simultaneous blocks and strikes.

Break free from an opponent's collar grip using Kodureo montong bakkat makki (augmented outward middle section block). Press your thumb into the back of his left hand and twist his wrist backward. Swing your left arm outward against his elbow to secure an arm bar. Pull the attacker's left wrist and rake his eyes with hwidullo makki (swinging block). Seize the exposed belly of his triceps muscles and jerk hard to rip tendon from bone. Swing the attacker's injured arm upwards and strike the exposed armpit with hwidullo-jabadangkigi (swinging and drawing technique).

Ancient Taoist methods have been used for millennia to lengthen and strengthen the male organ to achieve greater sexual satisfaction for couples. Using the air swallowing technique, air is forced down into the stomach and abdominal muscles in stages into the penis, and the middle three fingers of the right hand are used to block its escape by pressing the perineal point mid-way between the scrotum and anus. The thumb and index finger of the left hand are made to circle the glans of the penis, pulling and jerking upward several times like in the kodureo montong bakkat makki to gradually elongate the penis.

To strengthen the male organ, erection is induced by massaging the penile shaft upward in a smooth circular motion with the left hand rotating the organ from side to side and then returning the hand to circle tightly around the base, locking the air energy in the shaft. Then the left hand is made to jerk forward, pushing the trapped air energy up into the head of the erect penis as in the hwidullo makki-jabadangkigi technique. This method is practiced as Solo Cultivation by the male alone to develop the strength and control before engaging in Dual Cultivation with a partner.

POOM EXERCISE NO. 88

The following sequence in Steps 16 through 20 involves the application of joint locks for which the eagle claw method is noted. These deal with the response to an attack which is preceded by a shirt grab.

Break the opponent's grip and crank his arm outward with your right hand. Push his out-turned elbow away, forcing his left arm backwards over his shoulder . Strike with the front kick into the mid-point of the former's left thigh to paralyze it. Then break his ribs with a punch. Knock him down with a leg sweep and grab his left leg in both hands . Rip his genitals with one hand, smashing the other palm against them to crush the testicles.

Ancient Taoist texts include methods of improving the sperm count by testicular massage to increase sex hormone production in the organ. One of such methods involves pulling up the male organ in one hand while using the palm of the other to gently tap and massage the testicles several times.

POOM EXERCISE NO. 89

The next technique of keumgang yop jireugi (diamond side punch) is shown in Step 21, where it is combined with an aerial technique pyojeok chagi (jumping turning target kick) in Step 22.

Block a kick with your forearm and strike his exposed groin with the right fist. Leap and twist in the air to smash his face with a target kick. Then push his arm upward and strike inside his exposed armpit, knocking him out.

In the wild, the majestic eagle can attack a poisonous snake, seizing it in its powerful beak. It performs a supreme dance of feints and agility as it side-steps or leaps into the air using aerial tactics to avoid its poisonous strikes while stabbing, crushing, and cutting the dying reptile's coils inside its sharp talons.

POOM EXERCISE NO. 90

Santeul makki (single knife-hand mountain block) in Steps 23 and 24 are performed in the back stance, which is suited to the speedy movements required for a throw and following joint locks often seen in the eagle claw methods. After stunning the attacker in Step 22, the defender inflicted another diamond side punch into his armpit pressure point.

Scoop his leg upward and turn him over, throwing him to the ground. Then mount his chest, pinning him down face-up and seize his left arm. Apply an arm bar by securing his left arm while pushing down on his left hand.

A couple may enhance the quality of their sexual intercourse by embracing while looking lovingly into each others' eyes. In this position, the man and the woman lie facing each other with their sexual organs connected. Each lover throws a leg over the other's, each supporting the other's head in one palm while the second hand strokes downward on the lower body of the other partner. In this posture of Dual Cultivation, both partners exchange, balance, and circulate their opposite sexual essence to attain higher levels of sexual enjoyment, spiritual love, and enlightenment.

PICTURE 35A
Dual Ki Cultivation Method For Couples

POOM EXERCISE NO. 91

Steps 25 and 26 demonstrate taesan-milgi (mountain pushing technique) which is a variation to the attack shown in Step 1. Once again, the defender is faced with aggression from an opponent who grabs his collar in both hands.

Swing both arms upward in a double arc to knock to expose his center line. Then use both claw hands to grip and crush both his trachea and testicles.

This technique involves a more advanced form of Dual Cultivation where the ki energy of the couple is made to circulate as one as they relax and harmonize with each other's sexual essence. The method here is a sexual position with the couple sitting facing each other on the side of a bed, each dangling one leg off the edge with their sexual organs connected. Like is placed against like, with their bellies and lips touching, as well as opposite palms pushing softly against each other. This allows the opposite polarities of Yang and Um energies in the man and woman to connect, enhancing the flow of spiritual energy between them.

KWANUM KA (SONG TO THE GODDESS OF MERCY)

(hyanga)
On my knees, hands joined,
I lift my voice in prayer
To the Goddess of Mercy.
I beseech thee:
With one of your thousand hands
Take one of your thousand eyes
And bestow it on your suppliant
Who is blind.
Ah, ah, in your boundless compassion
Hear my prayer.

NOTES

_____

_____

_____

_____

_____

_____

_____

_____

_____

_____

_____

_____

_____

CHAPTER 16

HANSU POOMSAE

PICTURE 36
Hansu Poomsae Symbol

Water gives life,
And ki is the source of life.
Water adapts to the shape of any container filling it from within
Ki flows with the fluidity and harmony through the channels.
Water reverses becoming wild and forceful without conscious thought,
Ki is an unbreakable internal power bursting out through the fists.
Hansu means water which sustains all things in the universe,
And this is the principle of Hansu poomsae.

To the Koreans, "Han" has various meanings, the name of the country, river, etc. The Koreans have described themselves as "Han." This has to be differentiated from the "Han Chinese," who are believed to be a separate race, migrating in a different era into present day China.

There are several rivers in South Korea, but only one of them has raised itself the highest into national consciousness, being noted for its numerous tributaries, its largeness or broadness, the evenness of its flow and waves, and even its sheer length. This is the Han River, the fourth largest river of the peninsula after the Amnok, Duman, and Nandong rivers. It is formed from the confluence of two major rivers, the Nam Han

212

River (South Han River), which originates at Mount Daedeok, and the Bu Khan River (North Han River), whose waters originate on the slopes of Mount Keumgang, receiving water from the Imjin River and several tributaries on its course to the Yellow Sea, bisecting half of the country.

The Han River also cuts through Seoul, the capital city, supplying its needs, and at its widest point, spans one kilometer with several bridges allowing vehicular transport across its waters. Its length totals 514 kilometers including its tributary rivers, the Bu Khan and the Nan Han rivers.

The "Miracle of the Han River" describes South Korea's remarkable transformation with exponential growth moving from a poor, underdeveloped Third World country to a modern first rate industrialized nation with one of the highest gross domestic products in the world. It also refers to the economic growth of Seoul, through which the Han River flows, and the period of Korean history between 1953 and 1996. This was only achieved through blood, sweat, and tears. The average Korean is taught to embody the values of hard work, education, and an entrepreneurial spirit.

Historically, the Han River has played other roles, including forming a bulwark to protect the southern tribes of the Korean peninsula from aggression and invasion from hostile tribes including the Mongol forces from the north. The three kingdoms of Paekche, Koguryeo, and Silla strove to control the river, as it was used as a trade route to China via the Yellow Sea. Each named it the Ugniha, the Arisu, and the Iha, respectively.

In its more recent history, the Han River also played another important strategic role in the life of the country. The year was 1951, at the height of the Korean civil war, when the city of Seoul was evacuated by its citizens and army in advance of the crushing onslaught of the combined North Korean and Communist Red army, which had enveloped it. The Han River bridge was blown up by American and British army engineers using explosives in a desperate attempt to slow down the approaching enemy forces.

The poomsae line is the Chinese letter that means water, and it is similar in appearance to single drops of water striking the same spot and subsequently running off to the sides as six separate droplets. Graphically, it would resemble six straight lines all meeting each other at the center. Six times Seoul was invaded and occupied by the combined Communist forces; six times it was liberated by the Allied Command of the United Nations' soldiers. These included the 1st and 8th armies of the United States military and South Korean troops, whose resilience was severely tested as they resisted, their fortunes of war shifting like the "to" and "fro" motion of large sea waves.

The first invasion occurred when Kim Il-Sung's North Korean army crossed south, invading on June 25, 1950 before being counter-attacked by General Douglas MacArthur at Incheon in September and pursued all the way back in a northbound counter-offensive. In the winter of 1950-1951, the Communist forces again entered Seoul, invading in December with a human wave of 237,000 soldiers commanded by the Chinese commander Peng De-huai. The Communists used a human wave frontal attack to overrun defensive positions of the South Korean military and their UN allies, an example which may liken it to a terrifying mass of an excited crowd pouring out of a football stadium. After the initial shock and losses of the battles that ensued, the South Koreans liberated their country in an east-west counter-offensive line across the Han River.

The third assault on South Korea, which occurred through the Imjin River, resulted in the temporary abandonment of Seoul. This was followed by a fourth Communist offensive on February 11, 1951, aimed at driving the South Korean army and UN forces into the Sea of Japan. On March 14, South Korean General Paik Sun-yup, heading the 1st Division, retook Seoul, pushing Peng's army back across the Han River and the 38th parallel line separating the north from the south.

Again, on April 22, Peng's fifth and largest offensive broke through the south's defenses utilizing 305,000 Communist troops aiming to recapture Seoul. Peng's offensive faltered within sight of Seoul before withdrawal north back across the Han River. From May 16 to 23, Peng launched his sixth and last major offensive. This was countered by the South Korean 6th Division near Mount Yongmun against heavy odds, the battle spurning incredible heroic acts like the exploits of Taekwondo expert Second Lieutenant Nam Tae-Hi, who, after losing his weapon, single-handedly engaged with enemy fighters when his unit was outnumbered, killing more than two dozen Chinese soldiers in unarmed combat. This last reversal of the fortunes of the Communist North Korean and Chinese forces led to negotiations on July 10, 1951, and the signing of armistice two years later on July 27, 1953.

The overriding philosophy expressed in Poomsae Hansu is resilience. Similar descriptions for this characteristic are indomitable spirit, perseverance, patience, adaptability, yielding, ebb and flow, reversal, rebounding, and following the currents. Just like a savings investment which is created with regular monthly deposits of small amounts made into an account ultimately yields a nice sum once the policy has reached maturity, a drop of water continuously gathers to make an ocean.

The overarching symbol of water in this poomsae is based on its importance as a form of energy reflecting on the above descriptions of "adaptability," "ebb and flow," and "following the currents." Perhaps this is why the following words have been attributed to the great martial arts legend Bruce Lee:

...Be formless...shapeless like water.
If you put water into a cup,
It becomes the cup.
You put water into a bottle,
It becomes the bottle.
You put it into a teapot,
It becomes the teapot.
Water can flow,
And it can crash.
Be water, my friend...

A deeper examination of the poomsae lines shows a striking resemblance to an axle with six spokes of equal length, the ends of which may be connected together to form a circle. In Taoist literature, this symbol is identical to the Small Heavenly Circle.

There is a strong similarity to the principles of the thirteen torso requirements of the Chinese internal martial art of Tai Chi, which in turn are based heavily on maintaining an erect spine to promote ki flow within the Small Heavenly Circle. These principles include the following eight methods: suspending the head top; suspending or tipping the crotch forward to lengthen the spinal column and allow the ki to flow up the Governor Vessel behind; holding in the chest; and stretching the back to facilitate ki flow down the Conception Vessel in front. The remaining four methods approximate the flexed fetal position, which is thought to enable ki flow from the umbilical cord through the body of the fetus and include: loosening the shoulders; dropping the elbows to allow the muscles give an impression of separation from the bones as the skeletal structure lengthens and rises; wrapping or nestling the crotch between the up-pointed knees; and protecting the upper abdomen with the elbows close to the midline.

These methods are further clarified by five essential requirements which seek to find the center of balance and further develop the lower danjun for ki storage. These include keeping the body upright to coordinate the upper and lower limbs with the torso and find the balance between the left and right halves of the body; distinguish substantial from insubstantial to determine the balance between the front and rear foot, leg, or hip as the distribution of the body weight changes during movement; sinking the ki down to the danjun by silencing the mind, relaxing the muscles, and using abdominal breathing; attentive eyes and spirit which follows the release of ki energy from the danjun and its upward rise to the head through the spine; and martial spirit where the internal energy is released spontaneously with full body expression without the hindrance of the mind or thoughts.

The sum total of these methods attempts to find the center of balance internally where Yang and Yin exist in equilibrium and enable ample quantities of ki to be stored and released spontaneously, unencumbered

CROWN POINT

(GV 20)

HEART POINT

(CV 17)

SPIRIT PATH

(GV 11)

SOLAR PLEXUS

(CV 12)

ADRENAL POINT

(GV 6)

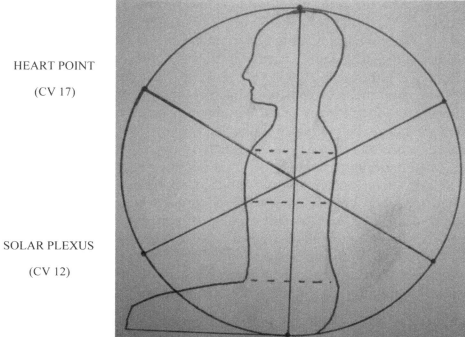

PERINEUM

(CV 1)

PICTURE 37
Six Axes Of The Small Heavenly Circle In Poomsae Hansu

PICTURE 38
Small Heavenly Circle Posture In The Human Fetus

215

by the thinking mind. Storage of energy is facilitated by visualizing the flexed figure of the human fetus as having two bows in the lower limbs with each knee as the handle and corresponding leg and hip forming the bow tips; two bows in the upper limbs with each elbow as the handle and both shoulders forming the tips; and a single bow of the trunk with the waist as the handle and the lowest vertebrae or coccyx and the top of the thoracic vertebrae as its tips.

In its final form, the waist becomes the handle of the bow and the knees and elbows form the tips of a single bow, coordinating together in the storing up of energy at the waist or danjun from where it may also be released upward or horizontally to either side.

More advanced practice focuses on the development of internal adjustments to form the magnificent posture which would be evident in all forms of movement. This involves separating the ki from the rational mind and sinking it downward for storage before transforming and raising it upward through the spine.

The Small Heavenly Circle is a central pathway through which the practitioner can navigate the body's ki energy, cycling, amplifying, and purifying it through the seven midline energy centers before final storage. The two main central meridians, the Governing Vessel and the Conception Vessel, are involved in this process, along with the seven major energy centers, namely the root or perineum point, the danjun, the solar plexus, the heart, the throat, the Third Eye, and the crown point. It is thought that the Yin energy flows upward from the perineum to the tip of the tongue through the Conception Vessel in front, and the Yang energy flows upward behind the spine from the perineum through the back of the neck and the top of the head to end at the Third Eye center. These two meridians are linked to all the twelve meridians at various points through which ki energy flows, acting as a central supply channel.

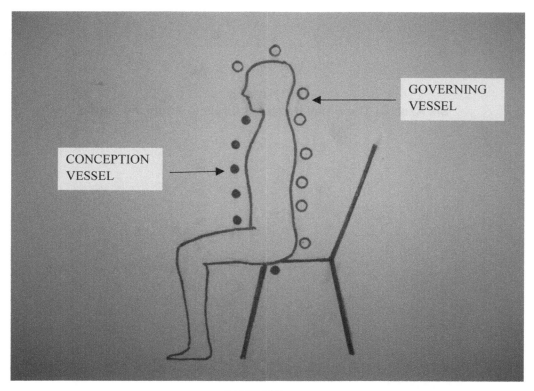

PICTURE 39
Conception Vessel And Governor Vessel Forming The Small Heavenly Circle

In the practice of the Small Heavenly Circle, the usual flow of ki energy is reversed by using abdominal breathing to cycle this energy up the spine behind to the head as Yang or hot energy and drawing it down from the head to the pelvis in front as Yin or cold energy. During inhalation, the practitioner uses the mind to draw ki energy along with the breath down the front of the body, cycling it over the tip of the coccyx and up the back to end at the Third Eye center, which is a point at the center of the forehead just above the eyes and which overlies the pituitary and pineal glands which are very important parts of the brain. In the exhalation that follows, the ki energy is again cycled downward through this pathway rather than being expelled from the body with the spent breath.

The vagus or tenth cranial nerve is achieving growing acknowledgement in humans due in part to its close approximation to the location of the Conception Vessel, the main Um or Yin channel of energy flow in the anterior part of the body. As the longest nerve and part of the autonomic nervous system in the body rivaling or exceeding the spinal cord in length, it arises from four nuclei of the medulla oblongata in the brain stem, coursing down the neck in the carotid sheath on either side between the internal carotid artery and the internal jugular vein to innervate all the major internal viscera in the chest, abdomen, and pelvis except the adrenal glands. Eighty to ninety percent of its nerve fibers carry important sensory information about the state of the body's organs to the brain. The remaining fibers send impulses from the parasympathetic nervous system to coordinate vital functions in the different organs.

Important branches of the vagus nerve include the pharyngeal and laryngeal nerve branches, the cardiac plexus, the celiac plexus, the inferior mesenteric plexus, and the hypogastric plexus, which approximate anatomically to the various energy centers of the body including the throat, the heart, the solar plexus, the danjun, and the root energy centers.

Vagus nerve stimulation increases the flow of saliva, activates the parasympathetic innervation of the heart to lower the heart rate, increases the secretions and peristaltic contractions of the gastrointestinal tract, and prevents asphyxiation by keeping the larynx open. This nerve is easily stimulated through vagal maneuvers like coughing, the Valsalva maneuver (breath holding with tensing of the abdominal muscles and bearing down in the manner of passing a bowel motion), or an excruciatingly painful stimulus. Stimulation of the vagus nerve with an implanted electrical device has been used successfully to treat depression and suppress hyper-excitable brain cells and control seizures in epilepsy patients. Abnormal function in the vagus nerve may manifest as dizziness and fainting from a low blood pressure or heart rate.

The second half of the autonomic nervous system is represented by the adrenal activation axis or sympathetic nervous system. This system is modulated from the limbic cortex in the brain including the structures of the hypothalamus, the amygdala, the pre-frontal cortex, and the thalamus, and it descends down the spinal cord to exit at different levels as pre-ganglionic fibers to form chains. These include the cervical chain of sympathetic nerves (C1–C8), the thoracic chain (T1–T12), the lumbar chain (L1–L5), the sacral chain (S1–S5), and the adrenal glands. From these sympathetic nerve chains, post-ganglionic fibers arise to supply the various internal organs, blood vessels, and sweat glands in close opposition to the parasympathetic nerves and manifest opposite counter-balancing actions to the vagus nerve.

Stimulation of the sympathetic nervous system allows the body to rapidly adapt and produce stress activity in emergencies like increasing the heart and respiratory rates, elevating the blood pressure, shutting off blood flow to the skin and bowel while shunting more blood to the muscles, and heightening the awareness of danger. Overstimulation of the sympathetic nervous system leads to excessive rise of Yang energy, which manifests as headaches, insomnia, and hallucinations, reflecting excessive build-up of pressure in the head. This is usually the result of tension building up anywhere along the Governor Vessel or the inability to circulate the Yang ki energy from the head down into the Conception Vessel.

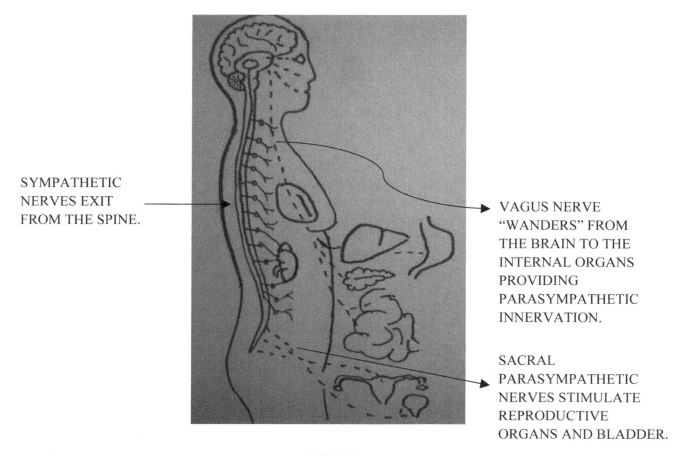

SYMPATHETIC NERVES EXIT FROM THE SPINE.

VAGUS NERVE "WANDERS" FROM THE BRAIN TO THE INTERNAL ORGANS PROVIDING PARASYMPATHETIC INNERVATION.

SACRAL PARASYMPATHETIC NERVES STIMULATE REPRODUCTIVE ORGANS AND BLADDER.

PICTURE 40
Sympathetic And Parasympathetic Nerve Pathways To The Internal Organs

The second half of the Small Heavenly Circle enables the flow of Yang energy up the spine to the head. The vital points on the Governor Vessel ascend from the perineum to the crown of the head and include the sacrum, kidneys, adrenals, and base of the neck, in that order. They occur posteriorly in midline positions that are identical to male sexual point, danjun, or navel, solar plexus, heart, and throat energy centers located anteriorly.

The diagram of the Small Heavenly Circle depicts a series of connecting points on the circumferential outline of the head and trunk when viewed from the side. These points are located on the midline of the anterior and posterior surfaces of every fetus, child, or adult, and represent the unified flow of ki energy within the Conception Vessel and the Governor Vessel respectively.

Its most undifferentiated depiction is as the saggital outline of the primitive fetus as early as four weeks old, when it has the amorphic appearance of a flattened bean with a barely distinct fore-brain in the upper pole, and an anterior surface dominated by the yolk sac and cecal bud, both structures which will soon transform into the umbilical cord. The beginnings of the midline gastro-intestinal tract can be observed arising from the lower part of the head, forming in the following order: a set of pharyngeal pouches, fore-gut, mid-gut with its attachment to the yolk sac, and the hind-gut, ending in the cloaca at the lower pole. At this stage of development, the primitive gastro-intestinal tract is still a midline structure yet to undergo the rotation of the mid-gut and closely resembles the Conception Vessel. The long curve of the posterior surface extending from the lower pole and rising up to the upper pole reveals the primitive neural structure which will ultimately be transformed into the spine. This may also be the equivalent of the Governor Vessel.

UPPER POLE

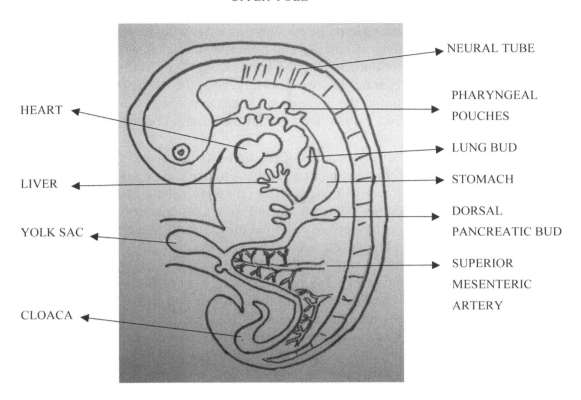

LOWER POLE

PICTURE 41
Connection Of The Conception Vessel Of The Gut To The Governor Vessel
Of The Nervous System In The Human Fetus

The tip of the tongue is the termination of the Conception Vessel which rises from the perineum below. The tongue, located in the mouth, helps to guide and swallow chewed food mixed with saliva. This is the first stage of the digestion process, which continues as the food passes down the esophagus into the stomach and intestines to mix with other digestive juices. Nutrients are extracted from the ingested meal to provide the vital food ki energy source for the body. This process is coordinated by a stimulating effect of the vagus nerve on the secretions and contractility of the bowel, and is enhanced by the massaging effect of the inhaled breath acting through the downward descent of the diaphragm to propel the products of digestion and waste through the intestinal tract.

The lung bud just below the pharyngeal pouches in the fore-gut further differentiates into the lungs while the splanchnic mesoderm around it becomes the heart. The triple heater includes the lungs (upper heater) which absorb ki energy from the air in concert with digestive processes in the stomach (middle heater) and intestines (lower heater) to process the post-birth ki energy. This energy derived from air and food is stored in the middle danjun, which is located at the level of the solar plexus.

The cloaca in the lower end of the hind-gut develops further into specialized organs including the kidneys, the bladder, the sexual organs, and the ano-rectal outlet, which are responsible for excretory functions as well as the storage of pre-conception and sexual ki energies.

The spine, comprised of the nine fused bones of the coccyx and the sacrum, as well as twenty-four separate vertebral bones in its length, extends upward to the foramen magnum to connect to the base of the skull. Within it is contained the spinal cord, spinal nerves, and the CSF. Also supporting the entire length of the spine from within and enclosing the CSF is a tough fascia derived from the dura mater, otherwise known as the posterior longitudinal ligament. Externally, the anterior longitudinal ligament and the supra-spinous ligament stabilize the entire spine along its anterior and posterior borders respectively.

The dural fascia of the spine is continuous with the dural lining of the brain, becoming the falx cerebri, a sickle-shaped midline fascia that separates the two hemispheres of the brain. This important fascia extends from the posterior pole of the cranium to the anterior pole, where it is attached to the frontal crest behind the frontal bone and below to the crista galli, a bony part of the ethmoid bone structure that forms the roof of the nasal cavity.

It is easy to appreciate the indirect connections of the tip of the tongue to the falx cerebri as it presses against the hard palate. Heavy rhythmic pushing on the hard palate can create small upward shifts in the Vomer or midline nasal bone, and ethmoidal bone with its cribiform plate and crista galli above.

Ultimately, after birth these structures will generate and store ki energy at five points in the Conception Vessel, including the throat energy center derived from the third, fourth, and fifth pharyngeal pouches, the heart energy center from the heart and lungs, the solar plexus energy center from the stomach, the danjun or abdominal energy center derived from the mid-gut and yolk sac, and the root energy center located between the pubis and the anus. The remaining two energy centers, namely the crown and the Third Eye points, are derived from the Governor Vessel in the fore-brain within the upper pole of the embryo.

When the practitioner contracts the pubo-coccygeus, which is the muscle that contracts spasmodically during sexual orgasm and can also halt the urine flow, this starts the process of channeling ki energy flow into the spine. Equally important is the act of pulling the anus upward and tilting the sacrum forward in that sequence. This sacral pump activity can generate piezo-electric activity within the posterior longitudinal ligament, which can be made to propagate upward through rhythmic spinal movement. The fascia of the falx cerebri can be activated in turn to generate this piezo-electricity through the action of the cranial pump on the bony sutures of the cranial bones. This can be achieved by pushing the tongue against the hard palate coupled with the contraction of the muscles of the jaw to create small compression and expansion movements of the cranial bones. This action is likened to a switch which connects the Governor and Conception vessels, allowing the flow of ki energy through both channels to create the Small Heavenly Circle. Once the energy flows at this point, it may be recognized as a tingling in the tongue or a gush of saliva in the mouth with a peculiar taste of sweetness, otherwise called the Nectar of Heaven.

The tip of the tongue helps in the appreciation of sweet taste, and when pressed firmly against the hard palate stimulates the nerve endings of the greater palatine and nasopalatine nerves which synapse with fibers carried in the trigeminal nerve or fifth cranial nerve. The taste buds on the anterior two-thirds of the surface of the tongue are connected to nerves that are carried in the facial or seventh cranial nerve, while the glossopharyngeal or ninth cranial nerve carries fibers from taste buds on the posterior one-third of the tongue and the vagus or tenth cranial nerve carries fibers from taste buds located on the back of the oral cavity. These interact with second order nerves located in the nucleus of the solitary tract of the medulla from where they are further projected to the amygdale and hypothalamus in the limbic system as well as the medial half of the ventral posterior medial nucleus of the thalamus and then onto different regions of the neocortex, including the gustatory cortex where theta frequency brain waves may be induced. An epileptiform focus or electrical activity in the insular and superior bank of the sylvian fissure of the brain may be sensed as a hallucination with a sensation of sweetness on the tongue accompanied by a flood of saliva secretion inside the mouth.

Theta waves occur at a frequency between 4 and 7.9 hertz and are the dominant brain waveform in random eye movement (REM) dream sleep. The theta waves also occur during trances and deep meditation beyond the border of the conscious world, allowing access into the subconscious part of the brain which is usually inaccessible. Other benefits of theta wave activation include an increased sense of energy, release from stress, improved learning and creativity, astral travel, and the development of psychic powers like telepathy, clairvoyance, and remote viewing.

Activation of the gustatory cortex also leads to stimulation of the vagus nerve, which in turn triggers the process of digestion from increased secretion of gastric and intestinal digestive juices. It also stimulates increased peristalsis of the bowel resulting in further churning and breaking down of the larger food particles to enhance absorption of nutrients with elimination of waste matter.

The other point where a bridge can be created between the parasympathetic and sympathetic nervous systems involves the connection of ki flow between the reproductive organs, the bladder, and the sacrum. This is performed using abdominal breathing and the diaphragm to massage the internal organs and bear down on the bladder and anus on inspiration followed by pulling up and tightening the anus as well as tilting the sacrum forward with the straightening of the spine on expiration.

Finally, the ki energy may be held and cultivated at each of the energy centers listed above using the mind, and ultimately brought into storage and sealed at the danjun, a process which is experienced as a growing warmth sensation in the lower abdomen.

The Small Heavenly Circle may also be important in the circulation of the CSF around the brain and spinal cord. The CSF normally circulates within the central nervous system separated from the rest of the body except at two main points, where it flows very close to the external body surface which include the cribriform plate at the roof of the nose and the cochlear aqueduct close to the inner ear. At these two surfaces, significant amounts of the CSF is absorbed and drained into adjacent lymphatic vessels which act as a valve mechanism to prevent the excessive build-up of pressure within the brain. The CSF is one of the three vital circulating fluids in the body, the other two being the blood and the lymph. There are similarities in the function of the cerebrospinal fluid and the lymph, so much so that some people consider them part of one compartment due to their shared properties. Thus in a healthy person, blood absorbs oxygen from the lungs, hormones from the glands, and nutrients from the gastro-intestinal tract, and is pumped by the heart around the body to supply the billions of cells with these vital nutrients as well as remove waste products of cellular metabolism to be excreted through the breath or urine. Importantly, major blood loss from the body can lead to death within minutes.

At the cellular level, the oxygen and nutrients derived from the blood are utilized in aerobic metabolism, an important biochemical reaction to produce energy as well as water. The accumulation of waste products and water within the tissues would soon lead to death if these were not drained away as lymph within the lymphatic vessels. These lead the lymph fluid through one-way valve channels to enter the central collecting thoracic ducts which end up in the sub-clavian veins located in the base of the neck, where it is once more transformed into blood.

The lymphatic system plays another vital role by helping to coordinate the immune system by transporting the white blood cells from the production centers in the bone marrow and storage centers within lymph nodes and the spleen to fight infections through the body.

There is ample evidence to show that CSF also flows into the peri-neural lymphatics from the cranial and spinal nerves as an important route of drainage, helping to transfer neurotransmitters to modulate the immune function. This CSF, which is thought to be closely related to the lymph, surrounds the brain and spinal cord, cushioning the central nervous system within the sub-arachnoid space of the rigid confines of the skull and vertebral bones while supplying nutrients to the nerve cells, transporting neurotransmitters and hormones, as well as maintaining the acid-base and electrolyte balance. Similarly, it acts like the lymphatic system by draining away the waste products of central nervous system metabolism. An acute rise or loss of pressure of the CSF can lead to loss of consciousness or death.

Cerebrospinal fluid is a clear, colorless liquid produced in the brain through a process of secretion by the choroid plexus inside the paired lateral ventricles or cavities within the cerebral cortex. From here, it flows down the inter-ventricular foramina of Monro into the third ventricle of the mid-brain and then enters through the cerebral aqueduct of Sylvius into the fourth ventricle in the brain stem. The fourth ventricle continues as the central canal, a drainage channel throughout the length of the entire spinal cord, which is enclosed inside the spinal canal to open up at the conus medullaris, the lowest point of the cord at the level of the first lumbar vertebrae. Here some of the fluid drains into the large, low pressure lumbar cistern reservoir of the lower sub-arachnoid space. In most adults above the age of thirty, this channel is closed, leaving the only other drainage points from the fourth ventricle into the sub-arachnoid space as the two lateral apertures of Luschka and the median foramen of Magendie.

Within the sub-arachnoid space, some of the CSF flows upward in a relatively high pressure superior circulation over the surface of the brain to be reabsorbed into the blood through certain structures called the arachnoid villi of the superior sagittal venous sinus inside the head as well as lymphatic channels. The rest of the CSF flows downward through two low pressure channels produced by the dentate ligaments that anchor the spinal cord at the sides to the lining membrane of the spinal canal, creating the anterior and posterior circulations. Up to twenty-five percent of the fluid is reabsorbed into the lymphatics within the spinal sub-arachnoid space.

There is evidence that stagnation of CSF flow leads to a deterioration of the brain's function, and is often associated with abnormal body posture with excessive spinal flexion or extension, causing obstruction to CSF flow throughout the spinal sub-arachnoid space or restricted respiratory function. The vital internal circulation of the CSF has been shown to be dependent on a person maintaining proper posture with relaxation of the shoulders which, together with an upright alignment of the spine, prevents the cord from lengthening and obstructing the sub-arachnoid space.

Another important factor is the vertical motion of the brain and spinal cord from the cardiac impulse. When the heart contracts the cardiac impulse is transmitted to the brain's arteries, causing a pulsatile expansion of the brain. This compresses the lateral ventricles to force the CSF out into the sub-arachnoid space and also results in oscillatory brain motion with a strong downward movement followed by a rebound in the opposite direction. The pulsations of the spinal arteries, which are uniquely capable of bi-directional blood flow, are believed to also assist the circulation of the CSF.

This vertical pattern of brain oscillation is also produced using abdominal breathing techniques. Expiration is thought to cause the downward movement of the brain and inhalation is associated with an upward rebound. Tucking the pelvis forward helps to straighten the spine and the pumping movement of the sacro-iliac joints generated by the rising and falling of the abdomen and contraction of the pelvic muscles practiced in Taoist breathing methods may improve the CSF flow in an upward direction toward the head.

Additionally, abdominal breathing causes an essential coordination of the three important circulations with an increase in intra-thoracic pressure, influencing the filling and emptying of the great cardio-pulmonary vessels, flow of blood through the heart, and its strength of contractions. Increased intra-abdominal pressure from downward displacement of the diaphragm affects the flow of the spinal arteries, and massages the abdominal lymphatics to augment the upward flow of lymph into the blood.

Some have compared the internal circulation of the CSF within the confines of the sub-arachnoid space to the Small Heavenly Circle, finding similarities in the importance of Taoist breath work to improvement of flow within both circuits. In people suffering from CSF stasis, the properties of the skin overlying the area of spinal obstruction have been found to be changed. This is associated with a tactile sensation of "drag" by palpation over that spot, which improves subsequently upon successful treatment. Yoga practice also includes similar breathing techniques to channel ki through the Small Heavenly Circle, and the belief that the Kundalini or the Yin sexual energy of the body which resides in the base of the spine can be released as a powerful upward flow from the base of the spine through the central canal of the spinal cord to the Third Eye inside the head.

THE TAO TE CHING

The supreme good is like water,
which nourishes all things without trying to.
It is content with the low places that people disdain.
Thus it is like the Tao…
Nothing in the world
is as soft and yielding as water.
Yet for dissolving the hard and inflexible,
nothing can surpass it.
The soft overcomes the hard;
the gentle overcomes the rigid.
Everyone knows this is true,
but few can put it into practice…

The jumbi seogi is again the moa seogi wen kyopson (left overlapping hands), which requires concentrating the ki energy in the sacral plexus or root chakra, which is the beginning and source of human life. This is in preparation to sink the ki down further and root the stances into the earth. Water energy with all its strength flows following the contours of the earth, rooting and uprooting each molecule as it gains momentum.

The proper stance involves keeping the body upright and lengthening the spine by suspending the head above as if by a cord attached to the crown. Drop the shoulders, hold in the chest, and stretch the back. Use the breath to sink the ki to the danjun and suspend the crotch by tilting the buttocks slightly forward and upward to complete the posture.

HYPERSTIMULATION OF THE VAGUS NERVE

POOM EXERCISE NO. 92

Steps 1and 2 use sonnal deung montong hecho makki (ridge-hand middle-section block) as an escape from a double wrist grab.

Flick out your arms dropping the elbows and step forward to unbalance the opponent. Counter-attack with du-me-jumeok-yang-yopkuri chigi (double hammer-fist strike). This involves pinching and twisting his nipples sharply to cause excruciating pain.

Avoid leaning the upper body forward and bring both elbows inside to protect the midline or upper abdomen with the forearms.

POOM EXERCISE NO. 93

Steps 3 and 4 demonstrate the rhythms of ebb and flow of water.

Step backward, ripping out his nipples with the santeul makki (single mountain block) technique. Then knock him out with a punch to the solar plexus.

This involves a weight shift from the front to the rear without leaning the body. The body structure remains undisturbed with the corresponding shoulder and hip moving together to coordinate the upper and lower sections. Send the ki down the Conception Vessel and up the Governor Vessel with a single inhalation to complete the flow of the Small Heavenly Circle and then on the subsequent expiration push the ki into the danjun for storage with the forward weight shift.

POOM EXERCISE NO. 94

Another variation of escape from the double wrist grab is demonstrated in Steps 9 through 11, where the defender uses sonnal deung montong makki with a forward step to break the hold.

Unbalance him by dropping your elbows, sinking the shoulders, and stepping forward. Hook your forearm around his neck and unbalance him with a sharp twist to his left side. Execute agwison khaljaebi (arc hand strike) to crush his windpipe. Then drop low and grip his testicles from below, squeezing them with du-jumeok jecho jireugi.

This involves being attentive to the weight shift as you pull him in with a left turn. Pay attention to your balance as you bring both legs together, closing the body posture. Send the ki through the Small Heavenly Circle with one inhalation, then exhale and sink the ki, wrapping your crotch between your knees to send the energy to the root energy center.

POOM EXERCISE NO. 95

Steps 12 through 15a follow the same template of liquid ebb and flow with abrupt changes in direction. This is achieved in the sequence of two withdrawal steps in low stances, pulling the opponent forward by his genitals using your right hand grip, and smashing his testicles with the left palm or the an-palmok-arae-pyojeok makki technique (target low section block).

Push your right knife-hand behind his left knee, scooping up his leg (sonnal keumgang makki). Step backward and force his upper body down with your left knife-hand. Twist to the right, pulling his leg at your hip, and thrust your left heel down into his face. Step backward with the crotch wrapped and release the stored energy by scooping up the opponent's leg above while pushing his body below to uproot him.

Energy storage requires internal adjustments with inhaling and closing the body as the ki sinks downward while energy release involves exhaling to raise the ki upward.

POOM EXERCISE NO. 96

The sequences seen in Steps 15b through 18 follow the rhythm of counter-attack followed by a change in direction to face a new threat from behind.

Use a defensive entry to block a swinging punch with your left palm, knocking the three Yin meridians of the lung, the heart, and the pericardium located in the inside of his wrist. Then strike the fourth Yin vital point of the liver meridian located in his neck with the jebipoom mok chigi (swallow form knife-hand strike). End the confrontation with a kick to the intersection of the Yin meridians of the spleen and kidneys in the groin and an elbow strike to the Spirit Tower Yang vital point of the Governor Vessel at the mid-spine.

This fighting sequence involves activation of vital points in the cycle of destruction: pericardium and heart (fire), lung (metal), liver (wood), spleen (earth), and bladder (water).

Send the ki flowing through the Small Heavenly Circle in a single inhalation, then exhale with a strong kihap to force it through the throat energy center for powerful self-expression.

This poomsae also recognizes that an opponent may be defeated by a series of targeted strikes which add up to disrupt the energy flow down the vagus nerve and cause serious internal injury. The simultaneous knife-hand strikes to the pericardium meridian at the wrist and the vagus nerve in the neck are followed with a kick to the lower abdomen or danjun, attacking vital points in the downward energy flow of the anterior part of the Small Heavenly Circle. The knockout elbow strike on the center of the spine disrupts the upward energy flow in this cycle to rout the enemy.

Similar sequences exist in Taegeuk Sah Jang, Palgwe Yuk Jang, and Taebaek poomsae, utilizing the jebipoom mok chigi (swallow form knife-hand strike) followed by mid-line strikes to the solar plexus.

POOM EXERCISE NO. 97

The defender swings around in a 180-degree change in direction to face another attacker in Steps 17 and 18.

Blind him with a left knife-hand side strike or sonnal yop chigi to the eyes. Grab him and smash his face with pyojeok chagi (target kick). End the fight with palkup pyojeok chigi (elbow target strike) to the head.

These rhythmic changes in direction and strikes bear a semblance to an unsettled water vessel with the waves created lapping both sides of the container alternately. The arm strike outward in the open posture during inspiration sending the ki energy upward while the following movements with the target kick and elbow target strike in the closed posture of the horseback stance involve sinking the muscles downward during expiration. The ki flows downward following the movement of the muscles.

Modumbal moa seogi is a transitional stance in Step 19 which is used in Poomsae Hansu as a build-up to the next step involving the release of ki energy through the hands in the agwison khaljaebi technique. An example can be found in a disaster where heavy rains causes a dam to fail once the rapid rise of the water level behind its walls exceeds its capacity followed by the sudden release of energy as the walls burst, sending tons of water cascading down, drowning everything in its path.

This transitional stance involves half-squatting with knees bent and moving the insubstantial or non-weight-bearing left foot to the right foot to form a closed foot stance and opening by pushing forward the substantial or weight-bearing right foot.

OH SE-YOUNG

The Han River flows
Into rice fields and gardens.
The river colors barley and cabbage in blue.
Snowstorms can't stop the River.
Rainstorms can't detour the way of the River.
The River encourages all creatures to lighten their lives.
Now, the River flows in silence like the Milky Way of the universe.

NOTES

_____

_____

_____

_____

_____

_____

_____

_____

CHAPTER 17

ILYEO POOMSAE

PICTURE 43
Ilyeo Poomsae Symbol

A point, a line or a circle end up all in one,
The oneness of the body, the mind and the spirit.
This is Ilyeo, the thought of Saint Won Hyo the great Buddhist priest.
And the thought of Ilyeo poomsae.
When the eye opens the state of pure mind,
All worldly desires are unimportant,
The ego submits and death is nolonger to be feared.
This is the ultimate ideal of Taekwondo practice.

The original name of Poomsae Ilyeo was Poomsae Shilla, named after Shilla, which was the first kingdom that unified the Korean peninsula into one country. The philosophy of Poomsae Ilyeo is expressed as the following: the body, the mind, the spirit, and the substance are unified into oneness…a point, a line, and a circle ends up after all in one.

The movement pattern of Poomsae Ilyeo resembles the outline of a flower, the Rose of Sharon, which fits the description of a point akin to its red center; a line similar to the stigma protruding from the red center; and a circle, meaning the surrounding petals of the flower.

In Korea, *Hibiscus syriacus* is the flowering plant referred to as the Rose of Sharon or Mugunghwa, meaning immortal flower or single-minded devotion. It has been much loved by Koreans for its attractive beauty, purity, and strength since ancient times. Of the 100 cultivars of this plant that are indigenous to Korea, the Dansim or flower with red center serves as the national flower of South Korea. It has strong vitality and is able to grow in unfavorable conditions. Similarly, the Koreans have often survived in unfavorable conditions, having to overcome difficulties and hardships from numerous invasions.

The Rose of Sharon keeps blooming from summer till autumn (early July to late October), a period lasting about 100 days, and may bloom between 2,000 to 3,000 blossoms on a single plant. Each flower blooms at dawn and goes by the evening, never blooming again at the same spot.

There is an ancient legend associated with this plant, the Legend of Mugunghwa.

There once lived a beautiful and warm-hearted woman. Not only was she pretty, but she was good at writing poetry, calligraphy, painting, and singing. Many of the men in the village were in love with her, wanting to marry her, but she chose a poor blind man. Everyone was curious as to her choice of husband when she could have had any man in the village. She was a good wife and took good care of him, going out to perform menial tasks without complaining, and her story spread wide, reaching the ears of the village administrator. The village administrator sent for her to see for himself, becoming smitten once he laid his eyes on her. She was so beautiful that he made a proposal of marriage which she immediately refused, being already married to the blind man. He pleaded with her, promising to do anything for her if she would marry him, and even tried to lure her in different ways. She refused and pleaded to go home, which angered him. He just couldn't believe that she would want to go back to a blind man and threatened to kill her if she wouldn't obey him. She cried that she would rather die than marry him, which angered him further. He immediately ordered her to be killed. Before her death, she made a request that she be buried under the fence of her house.

The following year, at the same spot where she was buried, a plant grew up surrounding the fence and gave bloom to very beautiful flowers. She was reborn as a tree to take care of her blind husband; this was called Mugunghwa or the Rose of Sharon. All the people thought the flower was the spirit of the beautiful woman who had died for her husband.

The Silla kingdom called itself Mugunghwa country and even the ancient Chinese referred to Korea as "The land of gentlemen where Mugunghwa blooms." The national anthem of the late nineteenth century mentions this flower: "Mugunghwa sacheolli hwaryeo gangsan" (Rose of Sharon, thousand miles of beautiful mountain and river land).

It is also fitting that the Grand Order of Mugunghwa is the highest decoration awarded by the government of the Republic of Korea. It is awarded to any individual who is serving or has served as the Head of State of South Korea and its allies, as well as their spouses.

The previous name for Mugunghwa was Cheon-Ji- Hwa, meaning "flower that indicates the sky" and the forerunners to the elite fighting force of the Silla kingdom took their name, Cheonji- Hwarang, from this flower, which they wore on their caps. These young warriors enabled the Silla kingdom to overcome the neighboring kingdoms of Kogyuro and Baekje, unifying the peninsula. Under the instruction of Won Kwang Dae Sa, who was a martial arts master as well as a Buddhist priest, the Hwarang trained rigorously and unmercifully to become invincible as warriors. They were so adept that even when they lost their weapons in battle, they were just as deadly with their bare hands and feet. They were drawn from the ranks of royal princes, noblemen, and other young men of good character and background, and were also schooled in the fine arts of literature, music, and art, as well as matters of government and state. Their lives existed for a singular purpose: service to their king and country. It was a state of perfect selflessness characterized by their five commandments:Sa-Kun-E-Chung (loyalty to one's country); Sa-Chin-E-Hyo (honor and respect to one's parents); Kyo-U-E-Shin (trust and sincerity in friendship); Inn-Hun-Mo-Teh (courage, never retreating in the face of the enemy); and Sai-Sang-U-Tek (justice, never taking a life without just cause).

There was also the Kyo Hoon Code, or nine virtues which the Hwarang lived by, and they included In (humility), Oui (justice), Yeh (courtesy), Ji (wisdom), Sin (trustworthiness), Sun (goodness), Duk (virtue), Chung (loyalty), and Yong (courage).

The most famous Hwarang of all was General Kim Yu Shin, under whose command the Hwarang were able to unite the three kingdoms. He was an outstanding martial artist as well as an expert swordsman. Legend has it that he was forbidden by his mother to spend time with his young love, Chon Gwan, so as not to be distracted in his training and duties. One night while asleep in his saddle, his favorite horse took him to his lover's house. Once he realized his mistake, he killed his horse and retreated to a cave to meditate and purify his body, mind, and spirit. As a result of his adherence to the code of filial piety and selfless dedication to his training, the gods bestowed on him a special engraved sword and several special texts of study which helped him to become one of the most skilled swordsmen and the greatest general Korea had ever seen.

The movement lines of this poomsae bear a close resemblance to another important ki energy pathway, the Large Heavenly Circle, traced from the crown of the head through the body's center into the four arms and legs and back to the original point. This circuit connects and regulates all the different meridians, opening up channels for energy flow into the arms and legs from the danjun. It serves as a complement to the Small Heavenly Circle, which uses Taoist breathing techniques to circulate ki energy up through the body's two midline supervising meridians, the Governing Vessel and the Conception Vessel, to concentrate and store internal energy in the danjun.

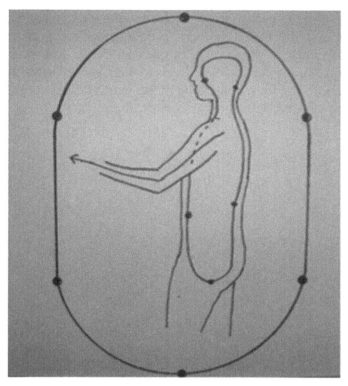

PICTURE 44
Large Heavenly Circle.

Poomsae Ilyeo teaches that a point, a line, or a circle end up all in one. It also describes the finger positions when used to trace and move the ki energy along the Large Heavenly Circle pathway on the body's surface. A single finger tip can be used to focus on a single point on the skin, or the tips of the middle three fingers are used together to draw a line along the pathway of energy flow, or the tips of all the fingers of one hand, including the thumb, can be brought together to form a small one-inch diameter circle over a particular area of the skin to focus the ki energy. Later, after attaining further expertise as a grandmaster, one can use the mind alone to enhance the flow of ki along the same pathway, channeling great internal energy into a limb, giving the practitioner almost superhuman power.

The essence of breathing in the Taoist philosophy involves the absorption of ki from the external environment and using special breathing techniques to coordinate its flow through the body. A well-trained practitioner is capable of releasing this ki energy from inside the danjun and is also able to circulate it through the body's midline channels, activating the seven energy centers located in the midline. Thus the practitioner can link the Governing Vessel behind with the Conception Vessel in front, completing the Small Heavenly Circle before directing the ki energy out into the limbs in the Large Heavenly Circle.

The Large Heavenly Circle is a complementary practice to the Small Heavenly Circle, where the cosmic ki energy is circulated from the crown energy center into the limbs after the opening of the Small Heavenly Circle. The starting point is the crown point on the top of the head, from where the martial artist uses the tip of the middle finger to trace the ki along channels down the front of the body to the feet and then up the back into the arms, finally returning to the starting point. A more experienced practitioner can trace the same ki through the same channels using the mind alone.

This pathway follows the poomsae line which represents the Buddhist symbol of the reverse swastika and bears a resemblance to the stellar constellations of the Milky Way. It focuses on the relationship of the

Big Dipper or Ursa Major, which is comprised of the following stars: Alkaid, Alcor Mizar, Alioth, Megrez, Phoeda, Merak, and Dubhe, and its fixed alignment to Polaris (the North Star). It is thought that the image of the reverse swastika is identical to the view of the Big Dipper at four positions in its counterclockwise celestial motion of 360 degrees around the earth's axis when viewed from the northern hemisphere. The North Star also is directly above the viewer standing at the North Pole and the Big Dipper can be seen making its 360-degree round trip around Polaris on a winter's night.

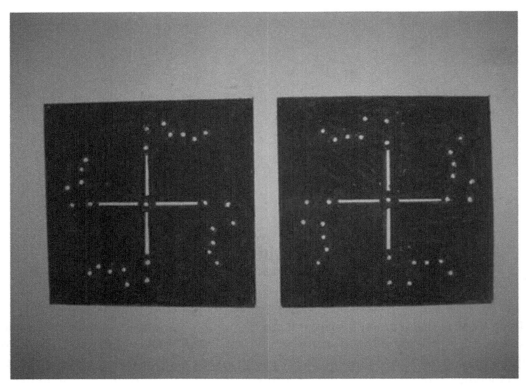

PICTURE 45
Big Dipper Constellation Positions Around The North Star At The Different Seasons Of The Year

Picture On The Left Is The Normal View From The Earthly Dimension
Picture On The Right Is The Reverse Image When Viewed From The Opposite Spiritual Dimension

The path of the Large Heavenly Circle is circulated on the practitioner's body and limbs after absorbing the cosmic energy at the crown point, similar to the heavenly forces between the stars of the Big Dipper and the North Star. This energy path is traced back to the crown point, highlighting the belief of the ancient Taoist masters that the human soul originated from the North Star and Big Dipper and to which it will ultimately return after death, completing its celestial journey.

A closer examination reveals that this pathway traces over the main muscles, muscle fascia, and tendons that execute flexion and extension actions across the important joints to maintain a proper body posture and facilitate the flow of ki energy into the limbs. Ki is sent down the main extensor groups of muscles of the trunk and limbs during expiration and returns through the main flexor muscles during inspiration as alternating waves that improve muscle and tendon strength and vitality. This is a process otherwise referred to as tendon washing or changing and allows the coordinated action of all the extensor groups of muscles to act as one in an instant, facilitated by the simultaneous coordinated relaxation of all the flexor or antagonist muscles.

In greater detail, the practitioner draws the tips of the middle finger of both hands slowly to the gall bladder lines one to two inches to the sides of the crown point. This symbolizes the opening of the aperture of the crown point through which the universal ki energy is absorbed and focused on the Third Eye. Then the fingertips are drawn along the tendon fascia or cranial aponeurosis at the top of the head and over the frontalis muscle of the forehead, simultaneously following this movement with the mind. Then the fingertips trace downward over the orbicularis oculi muscles that shut the eyes, then the zygomaticus, the buccinators, and the orbicularis oris muscles that control the cheeks and lips as well as the masseters that clench the jaws. The above muscles together with the muscles of the tongue act to squeeze the cranial bone sutures and activate the cranial pump enabling the CSF to flow upward. Both hands come together along the center of the throat to the base of the neck following the midline of the platysma muscle, which acts to flex and tense the neck.

From this point both hands separate, moving outward to the center of the clavicles, and then downward over the nipples, crossing the muscles of expiration to meet the groin crease on both sides. These include the internal intercostals between the ribs, the rectus abdominus, and the oblique muscles as well as the tranversus abdominus in the anterior abdominal wall.

Each hand continues downward, tracing along the iliopsoas muscle or hip flexor located below the midpoint of the inguinal ligament, then the knee flexors which include the quadriceps femoris and sartorius muscles at the top of the thighs. It continues downward, passing the inside of the thick fascia of the patella tendon in the knees and the ankle flexors, passing over the tendons of the tibialis anterior, extensor hallucis longus, and peroneus muscles in the inside of the ankle, to end at the base of each big toe. When using the mind to trace the ki energy, this first phase is carried out during expiration.

The second phase, performed during inspiration, describes the upward movement of the ki which starts at the Bubbling Well point in the center of the plantar fascia or sole of the foot. The practitioner touches this point with the tip of the middle finger and draws the fingertips from below to brush the side of the little toe

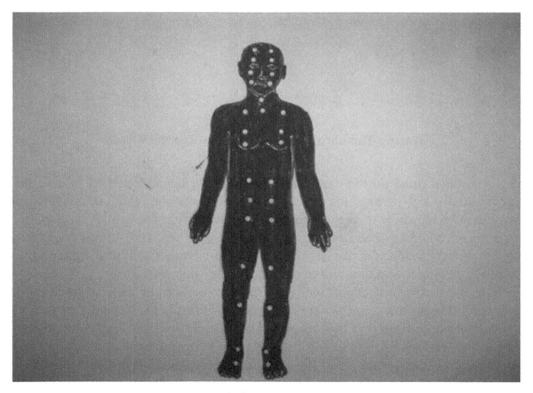

PICTURE 46
Tracing The Large Heavenly Circle- First Phase.

before continuing along the outer part of the foot past the side of the ankle to follow the Achilles tendon up the soleus and gastrocnemius calf muscles before crossing the knee and hamstrings or knee extensor muscles to the hip joint.

The ki is led further under the hip extensors or gluteus muscles in the cheeks of the buttocks to its mid-line before ascending up the extensors of the spine, including the erector spinae in the back, to the highest point each hand can reach. At this juncture the martial artist switches his palms to clasp either shoulder in turn with both hands, using the mind to link the ki from the former points to the new positions of the tips of the middle fingers and draws the ki up to the back of the shoulders.

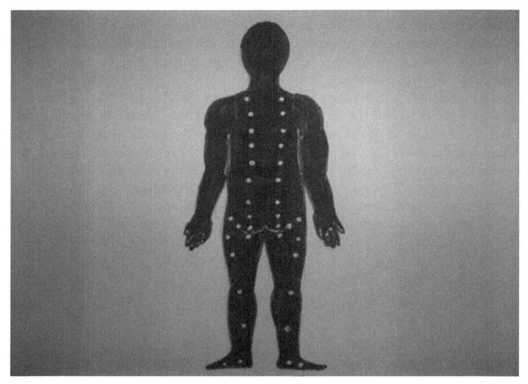

PICTURE 47
Tracing The Large Heavenly Circle- Second Phase

In the third phase, performed during expiration, the ki is further directed by tracing the tip of middle finger of the right hand around the muscles attached to the left scapula, which rotates the left arm outward, and down the left elbow extensor or triceps muscle in the outer part of the arm. As it flows past the elbow it continues over the muscles and tendons of the extensors of the left hand to the center of the strong extensor retinaculum fascia in the wrist. Then it reaches over the tendons in the back of the hand to the side, moving across the tip of the little finger to end at the tip of the middle finger.

The fourth phase, performed in inspiration, involves using the right hand to trace the ki energy from the tip of the left middle finger through the palmar aponeurosis fascia in the center of the palm, which connects the flexor tendons of the fingers. The ki is pulled upward through the carpal ligament inside the wrist and then outward to the tendons of the brachio-radialis muscle near the radial artery pulse. From here, the right hand leads the ki upward over the wrist flexors to the crease of the left elbow, passing over the biceps muscle and other elbow flexors in the inside of the arm to end at the front half of the deltoid muscle in the left shoulder.

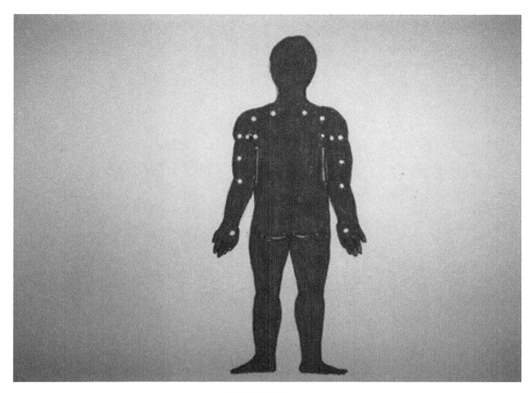

PICTURE 48
Tracing The Large Heavenly Circle-Third Phase

The same process is repeated using the left hand to lead the ki into and away from the right upper limb in turn. Finally, both hands resume the ki circulation by tracing up the trapezius muscles or neck extensors located at the sides of the cervical vertebrae to the base of the skull and over the occipitalis muscle with its cranial aponeurosis in the back of the head to end at the top of the head. The fingertips are brought together in the midline to the crown point to close the opening to the Third Eye.

This completes the Large Heavenly Circle and involves directing the ki energy along the vital points of all the major meridians except the heart and the Governor channels. The ki is then directed down the front of the body in the Small Heavenly Circle and stored in the danjun.

The experienced martial artist can complete the whole circuit in two breaths. Exhalation is used to send the ki down from head across the flexor muscles of the trunk and lower limbs to the feet and inhalation is used to draw it up from the feet through the extensors of the lower limbs and the spine to the shoulders. The next exhalation pushes the ki into the extensors of the upper limbs ending in the fingers, followed by an inhalation pulling the energy from the fingers through the flexors of the upper limbs.

This system of ki circulation throughout the body utilizes the Eight Extraordinary Meridians which include the four "Primary Vessels," namely the Conception, the Governor, the Thrusting, and the Belt channels, linked with the four "Secondary Vessels," namely the Yang Linking, the Yin Linking, the Yang Heel, and the Yin Heel channels. The latter four have no separate points of their own, instead criss-crossing the twelve organ meridians to link them in a vast network of the ki energy system.

Eight separate "master" and "coupled" points on these eight vessels are located within the network and can be accessed with the tip of the index finger in set combination to activate the flow of this energy system. These are identified as "Master" and "Coupled" points of each other and are located either in the hand or foot in each pair.

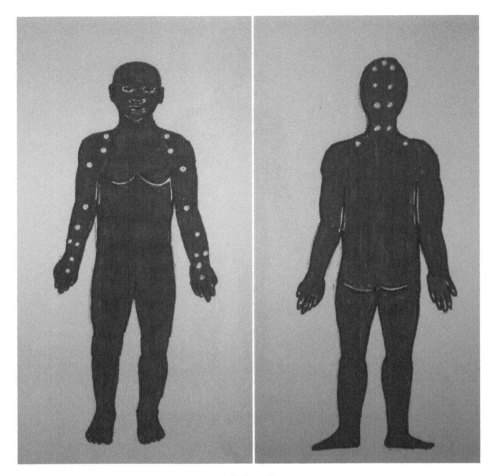

PICTURE 49
Tracing The Large Heavenly Circle-Fourth Phase

Small Intestine 3 (Governor Vessel) is on the outer edge of the palm and is paired with Bladder 62 (Yang Heel Vessel) below the lateral malleolus of the ankle. Lung 7 (Conception Vessel) is over the radial arterial pulse on the inside of the wrist and is paired with Kidney 6 (Yin Heel Vessel) below the medial malleolus of the ankle. Gall Bladder 41 (Belt channel) is on the outer part of the mid-foot and is paired with Triple Heater 5 (Yang Linking Vessel) below the middle of the outer part of the wrist. Spleen 4 (Thrusting channel) is on the inner part of the mid-foot and is paired with Pericardium 6 (Yin Linking Vessel) below the middle of the inner part of the wrist.

The symbol of Poomsae Ilyeo is the Buddhist mark of the reverse swastika, which has metaphysical roots and philosophy: the state of spiritual cultivation is said to be "Ilyeo" (Oneness), in which the body and the mind, I (the subject) and you (the object), the spirit and the substance are unified into oneness. It means that one derives the state of pure mind from profound faith, namely the state in which one has discarded all worldly desires. To enter into Ilyeo is to enter another world where one no longer has any fears nor cares about death. The warrior fights as if embracing death, holding nothing back as he strikes with fearlessness. Yet this seemingly reckless embrace brings life as his mind remains crystal clear and he is able to overcome the enemy's every strike.

This is illustrated in the story of Saint Wonhyo(617-686 C.E), korea's pre-eminent Buddhist scholar who was once a member of the Hwarang. Once on a trip to China along with a friend Master Uisang seeking further learning, he took refuge from strong winds and heavy rain in an underground shelter at night where he suffered from thirst. Wonhyo drank from a bowl of refreshing water in the darkness and had a restful night. Once it was daylight, he was shocked to see that they had spent the night in a burial chamber and he had inadvertently drank putrid water collected inside a skull. They were forced to spend another night there because of the unrelenting rain and he promptly fell sick suffering from the terrifying sounds and torment of the ghosts of the dead .Later on deeper reflection, he saw that it was the fears and illusions in his mind that brought on the sickness. From this experience, his great awakening was stated in the manner below:

> Sleeping inside an underground shelter yesterday, I was at ease,
> But sleeping inside a tomb last night, my mind was greatly agitated.
> Now I understand -when a thought arises all dharmas arise,
> And when a thought disappears, the shelter and grave are one and the same.
> The Three Worlds exist simply in the mind.
> And all phenomena are mere perception.
> Since there is no Dharma outside the mind,
> How can it be sought for elsewhere?

The reverse swastika's implied leftward direction or spinning motion reveals the key to this ability to switch into a world of nirvana. The familiar natural world, filled with its pleasures, pains, hopes, and disappointments, is associated with the clockwise rotation of the earth (from east to west). On the other hand is the other world of spiritual dimensions where no fear abounds and the spirit is capable of unlimited knowledge, boundless travel, and peace. This is accessed through anti-clockwise rotation, or from west to east. In several cultures worldwide, devotees usually use vigorous dances including repetitions of leftward directional spins and twirls like dervishes aimed at invoking trance-like states and communication with the supernatural world.

According to *The Secret Doctrine II*, "The reverse swastika conveys the union of spirit and matter, and is the master key that opens the door of every science, physical and spiritual. It symbolizes the human existence as the circle of life circumscribes the four points of the cross which represent in succession birth, life, death, and immortality…"

In Taekwondo poomsae, this state of mind is called mushim and is only achieved when one can calm both mind and body, slipping into a state of full relaxation devoid of nervous energy. Fear energy brings on arousal in the limbic cortex, but can be manipulated by meditative breathing to induce mushim or a state of no thought. Likewise, a cornered animal no longer experiences fear of pain or death, becoming single-minded and dangerous in its determination to fight back. Therefore, the movement lines of Poomsae Ilyeo represent the harmonization of spirit and body, which is the essence of martial art, after a long training of various types of techniques and spiritual cultivation for completion of Taekwondo practice.

The philosophy of Poomsae Ilyeo is expressed as the following: the body, the mind, the spirit, and the substance are unified into oneness… A point, a line, a circle ends up after all in one. This aptly describes the form of the Third Eye in its fully open state.

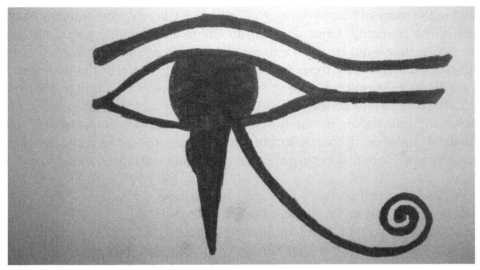

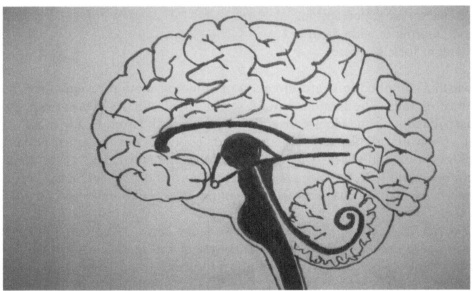

PICTURE 50
A Point, A Line And A Circle End Up All In One(The Third Eye)

THE BUDDHA SUMMARIZES THE TEACHING OF THE AWAKENED

To refrain from evil,
To achieve the good,
To purify one's own mind
This is the teaching of all Awakened Ones.

The ki rises with the CSF through the central canal of the spinal cord to reach the third ventricle in the mid-brain. Here it sets off harmonic vibrations in the pineal and pituitary glands, resulting in the fusion of the Um energy of the pineal gland with the Yang energy of the pituitary gland and the opening of the Third Eye. Once open, it is able to absorb cosmic energy which has penetrated through the crown point, raising the consciousness further with the spiritual awakening and enlightenment of the practitioner.

This bears remarkable similarity to various near-death experiences from different cultures where there is the recollection of the person's soul or spirit form separating from the dying body and being drawn through a long dark corridor or tunnel. At the other end is the usual description of an unearthly brightness opening into an infinite expanse of pure heavenly love, joyous peace, celestial music, and spiritual omnipotence. Afterward, the person is usually most reluctant to return from such a heavenly experience.

The first technique in this poomsae is the standing meditation or jumbi seogi, performed as the bo-jumeok moa seogi or right fist wrapped in the left palm, which allows spiritual energy to flow freely from the legs and upward through the body, attaining a harmonization of mind, body, and spirit. The martial artist is armed with a special power which can be used to dispose of an adversary or be used to channel ki to heal a sick person. In this technique, ki energy is drawn into, concentrated, and stored in the right fist, which is covered by the open left palm. This stored ki energy may be subsequently released by the martial artist for healing purposes.

The poomsae illustrates a series of various unarmed defenses against knife attacks. In this matter of life and death when there is no avenue of escape, one must accept the real risk of serious injury or that death is a possibility. To choose to live is to embrace death, and once the defender is no longer encumbered by the fear of being cut, then he or she becomes single-minded in the effort to overcome the armed assailant.

POOM EXERCISE NO. 98

Sonnal-olgul-makki (high section double knife-hand block) shows a possible response when the defender is faced by attacker who plunges a dagger down at his chest in Steps 1 and 2.

Step forward and grab the attacker's hand in both hands, halting its downward stroke. Squeeze the attacker's Union Valley vital point to weaken the attacker's grip on the knife. Then apply a wrist lock and twist the opponent's weapon hand behind his back. Knock him backward and off balance by thrusting your left arm against his neck. Thrust your body forward, pushing the attacker's own knife into his back.

POOM EXERCISE NO. 99

Steps 3 through 6 reveal the response when an enemy grabs you from behind with his knife held at your throat.

Push the knife away and break free from his grip using keumgang makki (diamond block). Then slip around the attacker's back, twisting his captured right arm behind him. Paralyze the opponent's Dispersing River Bed vital point with a strike and disarm him. Trip and pin him to the floor with ogeum- hakdari-seogi (knee back crane stance). Thrust the opponent's knife into his spine to finish him.

Steps 3 through 6 demonstrate the five essential requirements required for adjusting the posture to activate the internal energy in Tai Chi. These include keeping the body upright even after the long stepping movement; appreciating the weight distribution between the front non-weight-bearing and rear weight-bearing legs as well as the shift in weight to the front leg with the long step; sinking the ki down to the danjun for storage prior to its release; showing sensitivity to the flow of ki energy internally; and finally uniting the flow of internal energy in the body, making the ki follow the mind with its spontaneous expression at will in any movement.

The mind can be made more sensitive to the ki flow, likening it to the imaginary strings that run through and suspend the joints of the dangling plastic model skeleton in a high school science laboratory.

The latter technique involving the knee back crane stance can also be used to draw the ki upward from the legs in the Yang Heel Vessel and focus the energy through the tip of the middle finger into another person's vital point to heal or overpower him. The ki circulating in the BL 56 vital point of the bladder meridian at the back of the right leg is made to bridge the GB 41 master point of the gall bladder meridian located on the outer part of the left foot. The ki rises through the Yang channels to the Small Intestine 3 point at the back of the left hand below the little finger and bridges the Triple Heater 10 vital point just above the right elbow point to reach the tip of the right middle finger.

When the intention is to heal the sick, energy flow can be directed from the fingertip into the depleted Yang ki flow through the stomach meridian at ST 25, vital point located two inches lateral to the navel on either side of the weaker person (the stomach meridian is the only Yang channel located in the front of the body).

This sequence involves the activation of the cycle of creation, generating increased Yang ki energy: bladder (water), gall bladder (wood), small intestine and triple heater (fire), and stomach (earth).

As a practice of opening the Large Heavenly Circle, the martial artist uses the mind to direct the ki down the front part of the body for the first part in exhalation (keumgang makki), and then up the back to the shoulders in inhalation for the second part of the orbit, to the arms (sonnal montong makki), hands, and into the fingertips (pyonsonkkeut sewotzireugi) in exhalation as the third part of activation of this pathway, and finally back to the crown point in inhalation (waesanteul makki or single mountain block).

POOM EXERCISE NO. 100

The technique of wesanteul makki (single mountain block) performed with yop chagi (side kick) in Steps 7 through 9 reveals the defender's response to being grabbed from behind by an attacker as his accomplice, armed with a knife, attempts to plunge it into his chest.

Break free from the opponent's hold to face the more serious knife threat. Break the armed attacker's ribs with your kick and seize his weapon hand in both hands. Disarm him with du-son-pyo (two opened hands technique) and bitureo-jabadangkigi (twisting and pulling technique). Then step forward and thrust the attacker's knife into his spine.

The Yang Heel Vessel is one of the eight extraordinary ki vessels and connects each leg with the other Yang channels, including the Governor Vessel. By exercising the leg, ki energy is made to fill this vessel and is pulled upward with wesanteul makki (single mountain block) to nourish the Yang meridians including the bladder, the gall bladder, the small intestine, and the large intestine, as well as the brain.

The eotgeoreo olgul makki (double X high block) technique involves the linking of the pericardium PC 6 master point, located below the front of the right wrist, to the lung LU 7 master point, located on the inside of the left wrist, creating a connection in the Um linking channel.

Bitureo-jabadangkigi takes the form of an inverted triangle, which facilitates the downward flow of ki energy into the body like a person pouring water from a vessel held high to wash and purify his heart. The ki energy can be drawn down and channeled through both pericardium PC 6 master points on the inside of both wrists to re-energize the weak heart.

POOM EXERCISE NO. 101

In Steps 17 through 19, the defender demonstrates moderation by not using lethal force against the attacker who holds a knife at his throat from behind.

Escape using the technique of keumgang makki (diamond block). Then slip around the attacker and trap his hands behind his back. Kick him from behind with the front kick aimed at his lower spine. Knock him out using twio-yop-chagi (jumping side kick) to the back of his head.

Bringing the defender's fists to strike the hips lightly on both sides clears any obstruction in the ki out-flow through the Yang Heel Vessel at the GB 29 intersection point of the gall bladder meridian. The jumping side kick generates ki energy which easily flows upward into the Yang channels and Governor Vessel.

As you can see, the movement lines of Poomsae Ilyeo are the same as the Buddhist mark of the reverse swastika, which reveals its metaphysical roots and philosophy: the state of spiritual cultivation is said to be "Ilyeo" (Oneness), in which the body and the mind, I (the subject) and you (the object), the spirit and the substance are unified into oneness. It means that one derives the state of pure mind from profound faith, namely the state in which one has discarded all worldly desires.

This is also identical to the conceptualization of the Taegeuk and Palgwe, which refer to the universal truth of the mind, the body, and the spirit, or heaven, earth, and humanity. Ilyeo refers to the unification of this deep philosophical trinity. It may be expected that after a successful training in Taekwondo techniques and philosophy, one should be able to recognize the potential to achieve the state of Ilyeo in each poomsae, from the most basic to the more complex ones. This is the basic objective in perseverance with the arduous, intensive, and often painful training of the dedicated martial artist.

HYESONG KA (COMET SONG)

(hyangga)
Long, long ago, a mirage was seen over a fortress
On the shores of the Eastern sea.
"The Japanese army is here," the people cried,
And they lit the signal fire.
Three proud Hwarang were visiting near.
The moon lit her lamp; the comet swept its path.
"Look, the Japanese comet!" one of the Hwarang cried.
The comet that followed the moon in rising
Followed the moon in setting.

NOTES

_____

_____

_____

_____

_____

CHAPTER 18

SUMMARY

Taekwondo poomsae should be practiced in the right order as each form is usually more comprehensive than the previous one. New concepts are introduced in succeeding patterns based on the expected progress of the student. Each poomsae performance should end on the same spot where it was started. Inability to return to the exact spot is usually deemed as evidence of the Taekwondo practitioner's poor skill and immaturity.

On the physical level, forms are simply groups of small combinations of fighting techniques with the second half being more difficult than the first half of the pattern and new sequences of techniques are introduced on the left side of the movement line.

The training in the Taegeuk and Palgwe poomsae introduce the student to the concept of Yin or Um and Yang, which are complementary opposites contained in everything in the universe. Closer study of the black belt poomsae also reveals that the various techniques and philosophy reflect the dichotomy of Yin and Yang energies.

The philosophy of Poomsae Koryo emphasizes the spirited strong will of the warrior as Yang contained in the Yin learned nature of the scholar and the first dan is expected to exemplify these to achieve the second dan.

Keumgang reflects the connection between quiet thought and strong action which are Yin and Yang respectively and befit the black belt's dignity.

The ideals of Taebaek are described as heaven or Yang and earth or Yin, and the Taekwondo practitioner is expected to seek the bridge between these two states at the third dan level after six years of black belt training.

Pyongwon depicts the opposites of peace or Yin and struggle or Yang. The latter should transform to the former after ten years of Taekwondo training when the person is now considered to have mastered the basic and complex techniques and is able to teach others. Thus, like the hard work in preparing the fields for crop cultivation, a bountiful harvest will follow.

Sipjin focuses on stability and movement as Yin and Yang energies. This may also be seen as freedom being the opposite of bondage. The black belt is enjoined to continue to develop his or her skills rather than to become imprisoned in a false security engendered by the feeling of high achievement.

In Jitae, the opposite attributes are energy absorption or Yin and release or Yang. However, both are intimately connected as the black belt is trained to take the energy flowing upward from the earth and strengthen his or her body before it can be released from the strong muscles. This process is the theory of power and its practical application may take about twenty years of study of Taekwondo.

The presence of an attack contained in a defensive posture is the emphasis of Chonkwon, demonstrating this by using simultaneous Yin techniques or blocks and Yang techniques or strikes. Many may believe that speed and power are mutually exclusive, the latter emphasizing the slowing down of the speed of the attack. However, Chonkwon thought reveals that actual power can be improved through the sudden increase in speed of the claw strikes.

Hansu symbolizes strength and weakness as Yang and Yin. Weakness is not to be judged as a negative as it manifests as adaptability or flexibility in tactics which makes the black belt very formidable in combat.

The harmonization of spirit and body which are Yin and Yang is the concern of Poomsae Ilyeo. The training of Ilyeo is concerned wholly with the spiritual development of the individual, and its movement sequences flow through only left side turns, marking it out from every other poomsae which contain balanced sequences of techniques performed to either side. Thus Ilyeo reflects a journey that leads the practitioner deeper and deeper in the metaphysical world, where every movement involves the fusion of mind, body, and spirit as one. Its successful application time and again is evidence that both forms of energy can meld and become one, enabling great feats of strength and endurance as well as maintaining the body's internal balance and good health. On a practical level, to achieve Ilyeo is to enter the state of mushim or no mind, which allows one to perform perfect self-defense techniques in actual combat with no hesitation and with proper timing, overwhelming power and endurance.

No poomsae starts with a right turn as its first step, and it comes as no surprise that Taekwondo poomsae movement usually originates with a left side turn. This usually means a left limb defensive technique is followed by a right limb offensive technique. To turn left is to enter a journey into a world of spiritual knowledge and attitudes including the inner mind of man, while the path to the right leads through the conventional world of external values.

One should consider that every poomsae entails at its deepest and most profound level the gift of a journey into the spiritual realm, just like when the great philosopher Sinsi Bonki, a son of the fifth emperor of the Hwanung Dynasty in 35 B.C., was allowed to observe the rituals of Heaven and obtain the Palgwe or Eight Laws of the Universe.

Using special rhythmic breathing techniques, active meditation with quieting of the mind, static and dynamic postures, and limb movements, one is propelled along the path of enlightenment that each poomsae conveys. Exit from the metaphysical realm has to be made at the exact spot where it all began, and the martial artist returns to the conventional world with deeper and more profound knowledge of life than at the start of the journey.

EPILOGUE

I have only begun to understand better the words of the different masters and grandmasters whose wisdom I was often couched and concealed as they tried to explain the philosophy of the martial arts. Fighting had its origin in the need to protect one's life, family, and property from others right from the earliest recorded history of mankind, and our bodies were made to respond to various threats in the same manner, notwithstanding our different races, cultures, and environments. It has always been either fight or flight reaction to any serious threat.

In the martial arts world it would be couched philosophically as flight or fight in reverse order. To avoid, ignore, withdraw, or flee from an armed, belligerent opponent who is intent on causing serious bodily harm or killing you is no act of cowardice, as you will improve your chances of living to fight another day. All creatures are known to play dead, disengage, withdraw, or flee from overwhelming danger if given the opportunity. In our world, this would be the equivalent of prudently avoiding certain known trouble spots where danger is easily sparked, using measured voice tones to soothe ruffled feathers, avoiding the consumption of excess alcoholic beverages which can imbue you with a high level of false bravado, or running away in the opposite direction to escape your opponent(s). It requires a measured head to quickly assess the odds of victory in a potential conflict and refuse a fight even if you are likely to win. In victory, you may still be likely to contend with the ghosts of revenge attacks from the aggressor's family and friends, litigation from the belligerent party especially if he was injured, or prosecution from the law if it is deemed that your response to the attack was excessive and persisted even after the attacker was neutralized. This is the wisdom and spiritual development which we should all attempt to attain in our training in the martial arts.

In the fight or flight response, there is a massive outpouring and flooding of adrenaline within your veins, leading to a rapid rise in your heart rate. As your heart is pounding in your ears, threatening to burst in your chest, this drowns out the loud sounds of the witnesses in that environment, shrouds your peripheral vision and cuts out the aggressor's friends who are standing to the sides ready to give a helping hand to their friend, chokes the breath in your throat, rendering you unable to utter any intelligent sentences, reduces the blood flow to your muscles which subsequently deteriorate in their ability to obey the brain's commands and are then only able to perform gross body movements, and finally interferes with your ability to remain rational, rendering you down to the level of a frightened animal. The value of the spiritual aspect of your training should kick in at this point as you use deep rhythmic breathing techniques to slow down your heart rate, ignore the clamor from the high adrenaline levels within, and remain in control of your senses.

In the extreme, you will need to fight when you are cornered like an animal, or when your life is threatened, or when a family member, friend, or even a stranger is in danger of being killed. Just like an enraged animal in a crazed fury, using whatever measure necessary to quickly end the fight in your favor. The main difference is that an animal may claw, scratch, and bite desperately. Martial arts training is scientific, relying on the strikes and pressure to different vital points in the body to subdue the opponent. According to Grandmaster Won Kuk Lee, the founder of the Chung Do Kwan, the main differences in the martial arts is the way the different vital points are attacked. Otherwise, the principles of fighting remain the same…hit hard and fast, subdue, and escape. Your initial response should be hard and damaging enough to turn the fight in your favor, allowing you to dictate the next few seconds of the encounter rather than resulting in a long, drawn out conflict in which your chances of being killed will increase. Taekwondo training is very unique because it includes valuable training in long-range kicking methods, which is manifest in competition sparring or kyurugi, albeit under certain constraints and rules to safeguard the fighters, and supplements this with vital short-range fighting techniques contained within the poomsae which are unrestrained and limitless, containing the repertoire of all techniques which are disallowed in Kukki Taekwondo competition to round up the training of the Taekwondo practitioner.

One cannot help but admire the genius of our forebears who designed the training syllabus of modern Taekwondo. The training in Kyurugi or full contact sparring helps to acquire the stamina and anaerobic endurance required to outlast multiple opponents, including the development of sharp reflexes and footwork as well as the ability to take a hit while unleashing your own powerful counter-attack. Coupled to this is the expansion of the repertoire of fighting techniques to include illegal grappling and highly dangerous strikes that are found in poomsae. Added to the syllabus is the training in one- and three-step sparring practice, Han Bon Kyurugi and Set Bon Kyurugi, which develop one's sense of timing in evading an opponent's attack while stringing together your own counter-attack combination. Rounding out this package is the confidence that is gained in the power of one's strike that comes from successfully breaking multiple boards and other hard objects in Kyeokpa. Thus it is the responsibility of the student of modern Taekwondo to ensure that he or she is studying the full package contained within the martial art to pass on the knowledge to future generations.

LOCATION OF VITAL POINTS

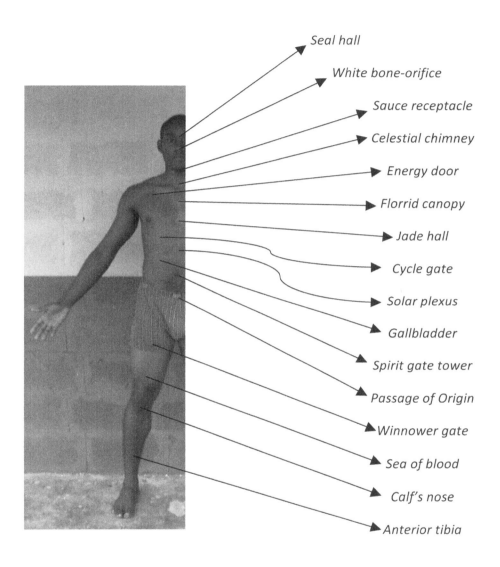

Seal hall

White bone-orifice

Sauce receptacle

Celestial chimney

Energy door

Florrid canopy

Jade hall

Cycle gate

Solar plexus

Gallbladder

Spirit gate tower

Passage of Origin

Winnower gate

Sea of blood

Calf's nose

Anterior tibia

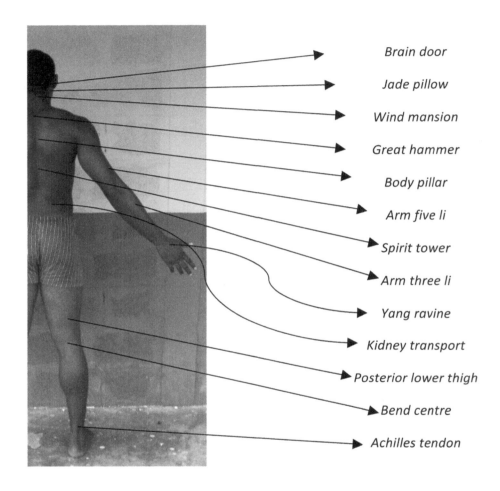

Brain door

Jade pillow

Wind mansion

Great hammer

Body pillar

Arm five li

Spirit tower

Arm three li

Yang ravine

Kidney transport

Posterior lower thigh

Bend centre

Achilles tendon

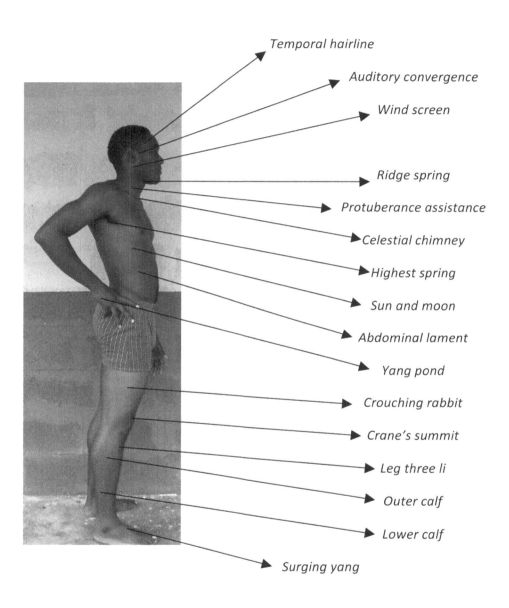

Temporal hairline

Auditory convergence

Wind screen

Ridge spring

Protuberance assistance

Celestial chimney

Highest spring

Sun and moon

Abdominal lament

Yang pond

Crouching rabbit

Crane's summit

Leg three li

Outer calf

Lower calf

Surging yang

BIBLIOGRAPHY

Chia, Mantak. *Iron Shirt Chi Kung 1*. Thailand: Universal Tao Publications, 1986.

——. *Healing Love Through the Tao, Cultivating Female Sexual Energy*. Thailand: Universal Tao Publications, 1986.

Chia, Mantak and Winn, Michael. *Tao Secrets of Love, Cultivating Male Sexual Energy*. Santa Fe: Aurora Press, 1984.

Cook, Doug. *Taekwondo: Ancient Wisdom for the Modern Warrior*. 1st ed. Boston: YMAA Publication Centre, 2001.

——. *Traditional Taekwondo: Core Techniques, History, and Philosophy*. Boston: YMAA Publication Centre, 2006.

Cho, Sihak Henry. *Tae Kwon Do: Secrets of Korean Karate*. 1st ed. Japan: Charles E. Tuttle Publishing Co., Inc., 1993.

Chun, Richard. *Tae Kwon Do: The Korean Martial Art*. New York: Harper & Row, Publishers, 1976.

——. *Advancing in Tae Kwon Do*. 2nd ed. Boston: YMAA Publication Centre, 2006.

Daniel, Charles. *Taijutsu: Ninja Art of Unarmed Combat*. California: Unique Publications, 1986.

Ha, Tae-Hung & Mintz, Grafton k. Samguk Yusa: Legends and History of the Three Kingdoms of Ancient Korea. Written by IIyon. Seoul, Korea: Yonsei University Press, 1972

Jeong, Byeong-Jo. Master Wonhyo: An Overview of His Life and Teaching. Seoul, Korea: Diamond Sutra Recitation Group, 2010

Kim, Sang H. *Vital Point Strikes: The Art & Science of Striking Vital Targets for Self-Defense and Combat Sports*. USA: Turtle Press, 2008.

Lee, Kyu Hyung and Kim, Sang H. *Complete Taekwondo Poomse*. USA: Turtle Press, 2007.

Lee, Peter H. The Columbia Anthology of Traditional Korean Poetry. New York: Columbia University Press, 2002

Kanazawa, Hirokazu. *Black Belt Karate: The Intensive Course*. 1st ed. Japan: Kodansha International Ltd., 2006.

Kang, Shin Duk. *One-step Sparring in Karate, Kung Fu, and Tae Kwon Do*. Burbank, California: Ohara Publications, Incorporated, 1978.

Mifune, Kyuzo. *The Canon of Judo: Classical Teachings on Principles and Techniques*. 1st ed. Japan: Kodansha International Ltd., 2004.

Nakayama, M. *Best Karate: Comprehensive*. 1st ed. Japan: Kodansha International Ltd., 1977.

---. *Best Karate: Fundamentals*. 1st ed. Japan: Kodansha International Ltd., 1978.

Novak, Philip. *The World's Wisdom: Sacred Texts of the World's Religions*. New York: HarperCollins Publishers, 1994.

O'Neill, Simon John. *The Taegeuk Cipher: The Patterns of Kukki Taekwondo as a Practical Self-Defence Syllabus*. 1st ed. Lulu.com, 2008.

O'Rourke, Kevin The Book of Korean Poetry: Songs of Shilla and Koryo. Iowa, USA: University of Iowa Press, 2006

Park, Dong Keun and Schein, Allan. *Tae Kwon Do: The Indomitable Martial Art of Korea: Basics, Techniques and Forms*. USA: Invisible Cities Press, 2006.

Park, Yeon Hwan and Gerrard, Jon. *Black Belt Tae Kwon Do: The Ultimate Reference Guide to the World's Most Popular Black Belt Martial Art*. New York: Checkmark Books, 2000.

Prentice, William E. *Arnheim's Principles of Athletic Training: A Competency-Based Approach*. 12th ed. New York: The McGraw-Hill Companies, Inc., 2006.

Stepan, Charles A. *Taekwondo: The Essential Guide to Mastering the Art*. London: New Holland Publishers (UK) Ltd., 2002.

Whang, Sung C., Whang, Jun C., and Saltz, Brandon. *Taekwondo: The State Of The Art*. New York: Broadway Books, 1999.

Lightning Source UK Ltd.
Milton Keynes UK
UKOW06f1837140115

244501UK00013B/391/P